W9-BYH-996

Learn To Value Your Childhood

Your History Is Your Teacher

Vince DiPasquale
with Mike Augustyn

A PROGRAM OF RECOVERY FOR CODEPENDENTS

NEW BEGINNINGS PUBLICATIONS

P.O. BOX 239
WILLIAMSTOWN, NJ 08094

Design and composition
by Dom Roberti, Haverford, PA

Title page illustration
by Sarah Browne, Pleasantville, NY
(age 6)

ISBN 0-9704461-3-6

Published by New Beginnings Publications, P.O. Box 239,
Williamstown. NJ 03094

2nd Printing, October 2009

Contents

Press Clippings

To thousands of people who have passed through the Delaware Valley addiction recovery community, soft-spoken Vince is a hero and role model. He has touched and changed countless troubled lives.

Camden (NJ) Courier-Post July 13, 2000

"I think the biggest thing that comes out of [the 12-step program] is you really feel a simplicity and you feel a serenity....I'm not interested in saving the world anymore. I'm interested in saving Vince DiPasquale. If I happen to help somebody else in the process, wonderful."

Philadelphia Inquirer May 5, 1991

Vince lectures regularly on personal growth, relationships, addictions, grief, and co-dependency. His message skewers romantic illusions and puts sexual attraction into a whole new perspective. But he delivers it with the timing of a stand-up comic, and spices it with anecdotes, sometimes hilarious, often profound, that ruefully recount his own struggles with overeating and co-dependency.

Camden (NJ) Courier-Post April 5, 1995.

Meeting Vince on your journey is like having an encounter with a good samaritan; he soothes your wounds and gives you help when it's needed.

The Healing News January 1996

"People learned a lot of rules when they were children," says DiPasquale. "Now they're learning that it's OK to make new rules as adults."

Camden (NJ) Courier-Post April 16, 1991

Preface

This book is based on a lecture series that I have been giving since 1981. To date, my audience has numbered well over two thousand people for each annual series. The Six Stages described in this book have been developed along with my lectures. They are based on principles that many of the lecture audience have found extremely effective in recovering from codependency and developing healthy relationships.

Further, the principles that I describe as the Six Stages reflect much of what is referred to as "leg work" in 'twelve Step programs, which are used today for a variety of psychological and addiction issues. They are called "leg work" because they give you something to do, in addition to traditional analysis and counseling, to keep your personal recovery in process.

The key to recovery lies in acknowledgment of the inner child as a potential source of playful vitality. Hence the title of this book: *Learn To Value Your Childhood.*

The process described here is one that works. I have seen it produce success time after time. Without hesitation, I recommend it to anyone who is experiencing patterns of behavior which are interfering with their living a satisfying life. To those who are willing to try it out, I say "Trust the process. It works."

This very special book is dedicated to all those wonderful teachers that the Higher Power has sent into my life. To my mom and dad, Camillo and Angelina DiPasquale, who were my first teachers and who gave me the gift of life. To my family, for all they have done throughout my years of growing up, I am grateful. Thanks also to the Catholic Church, which protected me through those years, and gave me a foundation of faith.

For all the people that touched my life during the 32 years when I was part of the priesthood, 12 years in the seminary and 20 years ordained, I send a sincere thank you for all they have taught me. Thanks as well go to all who have been instrumental in my recovery, and to those who guided me and were my mentors all those years. To Starting Point and its original board members, who came into my life in 1977 to alter my journey, another thank you.

A special dedication goes to my wonderful wife, Carol, my best friend and teacher, a gift that God has given me and with whom I am allowed to share my life, being my inspiration and my strength. To Denise, Diane and Michele, three special ladies with whom I have had the privilege and honor to share in their lives, I thank for accepting me and for all that we share. A special thank you goes to my seven new teachers, my grandchildren Bryce, McKinsey, Madison, Cole, Casey, Zachary and Jordan, who have been shining examples of simplicity, honesty, openness and willingness. We read in the Scriptures that, "a little child shall lead us". Being "Papa Vince" to these beautiful children has been an enriching spiritual experience. I would also like to dedicate this book to my new community at Holiday City in Williamstown, a place where people care and look for each other.

Some additional thanks are due to the people who helped in the birthing of this book. I would like to thank Mike Augustyn for essentially turning my lecture notes into this book and for making contributions to the text from his own and others' experience. To Dom Roberti, college professor turned desktop publisher, along with his wife, Carole, a sharp-eyed proofreader, I owe thanks for the design and composition of this book. To their grandaughter, Sarah Browne, age 6, I am grateful for the cover illustration.

Introduction

The purpose of this book is twofold. First, it explores codependency and shows how it virtually guarantees that our relationships will not work. Second, and most important, it gives a simple formula for breaking the bondage of codependency. The formula is something I developed over time, taken from many sources. I call it the Six Stages of Recovery. I share it with groups who attend a series of lectures I give. At this writing, I have presented this series for more than fifteen years, to well over twenty thousand people. My experience with them indicates that the formula works—if you work it. In this case, "simple" doesn't necessarily mean easy. But it does mean "effective."

One of the sources the formula is taken from is the Twelve Steps of Alcoholics Anonymous. If you are not familiar with the Steps, don't let the association with AA turn you off. And don't let the use of terms like "recovery" and "addiction" throughout this book turn you off either. Even if your "drug of choice" is not alcohol or some other substance, we all have a "drug": overeating, sex addiction, spending addiction, control, negativity....We have a long list to choose from, and most of us codependents have more than one. As will be explained, the principles of the Twelve Steps have now come to be accepted by mainstream psychology as effective in dealing with our drugs of choice, our codependency. Codependency creates insanity in our lives. We then carry this insanity into our relationships—and wonder why our relationships don't work!

The theme of this book is that codependency destroys relationships by destroying individuals. These individuals—*us*—are then like broken or incomplete people. We get into relationships looking for somebody else to make us whole. The point we miss is that *only we can make ourselves whole*. Getting into a relationship with another person, with a group, with a job, a religion, or any other organization will not make us whole and healthy. In fact, that's like putting the cart before the horse. We should be whole and healthy first, then enter relationships to share and grow further.

Finally, I said above that the formula will work if you *work* it. I have never known anyone who achieved their recovery from codependency solely by working it out in their heads. In fact, if you have tried therapy or know people who tried therapy to get their lives in order, you might be familiar with the common complaint. They *know* so much about themselves and their problems—yet their lives are no happier. Why? Because our codependency problems are not mental. They are not existential or philosophical or matters of religion and faith. They are emotional. They involve feelings. And your feelings start in your heart and sink into your gut, not into your head. So you cannot stay in your head and work things out; you cannot intellectualize your personal recovery. Therapy is a good place to start, and a good place to continue to grow—if you are willing to *practice* what you learn. This book is essentially about practice. Learn. Then do. Make yourself whole and happy, and the rest—including your relationships—will take care of itself.

1

What is Codependency?

PROBLEMS WITH DEFINITIONS

In dealing with our own issues and personal growth—which we call the "recovery" process—many of us have a problem with the term "Codependency." For some, it is a difficult term to understand, to get a *feel* for. Yet it is important that we do get a feel for the term, because it will be used to describe many of the problems we are experiencing. It is a label. Putting a label on problems helps us understand them. Understanding helps us deal with them.

If you are one of those having difficulty with the term, my advice is not to worry about it. Work on your growth and the understanding will come. Codependency is not the only psychological term that people have problems with. I know of a case of a person who was constantly obsessing, yet when he was told this he had no idea what "obsessing" meant, and it took time for him to get it. The same with the case of a person who lacked intimacy in his marriage. He thought intimacy equated to a sexual relationship, and he had that with his wife, so how was he lacking "intimacy?"

It is estimated that there are well over 400 books on codependency—and just as many definitions of the word. So if you're confused, join the club. But for purposes of this book, I'm going to offer a simple, personalized definition of codependency:

> **I am a codependent
> if any person, place, or thing
> that I am dependent on
> creates unmanageability
> or insanity in my life.**

Also for purposes of this book, I'm going to refer to codependents as "we," since most people are. And I would also like to get one other thing straight: codependency is an addiction. To borrow a popular term, it might be called the Mother of all addictions, since it appears at the root of all other addictions. As an addiction, it is not something we suddenly cure and then forget about. The treatment process—recovery—is an ongoing thing. To borrow from the Twelve Step Program of recovery, we look for **progress, not perfection**. The good news is that progress can mean happiness, peace in our lives. Drinking, drugs, obesity, anxiety, depression...and all the rest of the insanity and unmanageability caused by codependency...can be put behind us—as can the inevitable failure of so many relationships we try so hard to build.

A HISTORY OF THE CONCEPT

The concept of codependency and how to treat it evolved over time. Prior to the founding of Alcoholics Anonymous in 1935, our society approached problem behavior with what I call a secretive mentality: Out of Sight, Out of Mind. For example, if you were incorrigible, what might be called a disgrace to your family, you were dealt with in a very simplistic way. You were "shelved." If you were depressed and dysfunctional, you were placed in an institution. Pregnant out of wedlock? Shipped off—maybe to

Aunt Louise in California, where you'd save the immediate family any embarrassment. Kleptomaniac? Prison. Even in the mental institutions of the time, where you might expect some insight into treatment, about all the patient received was medication—numbed with different drugs and left to shuffle through life like a robot. It was enough in all of these cases if you were left to merely physically function.

It was only after AA, in the 1930's and 40's, that we finally made a grudging concession to a new mentality. With alcoholism, at least, we acknowledged the concept of addiction. But society still saw it as an evil, a lack of will power, a moral defect. Why? Because it challenged the only solution society could think of: CONTROL.

Maybe it's understandable that society had that attitude. If it had really accepted the idea that an addiction was a disease and not merely a character flaw, it would have felt obligated to offer an effective treatment rather than censure to the addict. And it simply didn't have an effective treatment.

What little progress was made with the concept of addiction as a disease almost disappeared after World War II—the period 1945-1960. As many psychologists call it: The Plastic Age. It seems that what happened was that the country, the world, had experienced so much insanity in the war that people decided there wouldn't be any more for a while. It was the old Out of Sight mentality, but with a twist. Society seemed to operate on a new slogan: A Place for Everything and Everything in Its Place. To see how it worked, let's look at two blatant examples: African Americans were "separate but equal," which meant that their place was in their own neighborhoods and schools, and own classes of jobs—menial mostly; the place for homosexuals was the closet—like the present-day approach of Don't Ask, Don't Tell—virtual denial.

Something else was created in this Plastic Age as well. The concept of what we can call "Sacreds." Ideals. Everything in that world was supposed to be ideal. Let me give a few examples. There was a slogan at the time: "The Policeman Is Your Friend," which meant that police brutality, in this ideal world, didn't exist. Another ideal was that clerics were saintly. They would never abuse children, sexually or otherwise. And we know today just how false that idea was.

The Plastic Age. There was no incest. Teenagers had no questions about sex and sexuality, so parents didn't have to suffer the embarrassment of discussing that taboo subject. Our country was always right in whatever policy it promulgated or war it fought. And so on. Plastic. Rigid. No questions. No feelings. There was a song at the time: "The Great Pretender." It might have been an anthem for the age. Because mostly everyone was pretending. *No problems here!* The absurdity of it was later summed up by the television comedy character, Sam the Eagle: "Man was put on this earth to work hard and do the right things." It was all so simple.

But the plastic cracked—or, more accurately, was *shattered*—in the 60's. All of a sudden the youth seemed to have a new anthem, summed up in the lyrics of a new song: "The Revolution's Here!" It was like all the internal pressure on society, all the denial and control, exploded in the youth. And they were iconoclasts. They destroyed the old idols, the Sacreds. With a vengeance. The police became cops, with a negative connotation. Homosexuals came out of the closet with Gay Pride, demanding to be acknowledged. Blacks fought for their rights—literally fought sometimes, with guns and violence. And half a generation refused to march to a new war in Viet Nam.

A new comic phrase was coined, a take-off on the old film, *Rebel Without a Cause—Rebel Without a PAUSE*. The pendulum of the Revolution swung too far. For example, where sex had been a taboo, it was now flaunted. The phrase was Free Love. It was promiscuity. Drug abuse was rampant. Timothy Leary, a *doctor*, led the LSD cult: Turn On, Tune Out was its slogan. The period has been described as a civil war. Young against old. Listen to the words of the songs of the younger generation of the time, the "hippies," as they describe the older generation and its lifestyle: "always the old to send us off to war, always the young to die"; "all made out of ticky-tack and they all look just the same." And they get worse. To the younger, the older generation became the

Establishment, the Military-Industrial Complex. Like the Evil Empire. If you want to see how hot this civil war got, at least in some people's minds, go to the video store and rent the movies *Joe* and *Easy Rider.*

But something good came out of it. By the 70's the pendulum was swinging back, and the older generation was saying that, hey, maybe the kids had a point. Basically, the shouting of the 60's died down and people were talking. They realized that the Plastic Age didn't work. And it was in 1983 that this idea was really given a jolt forward. It came in the form of a book, *Adult Children of Alcoholics*, by Janet Geringer Woititz. It was courageous. A rendition of what it was like growing up in an alcoholic home. It made the *New York Times* Best Seller List. A lot of people saw themselves in it. All of a sudden they realized that they weren't alone—and weren't crazy.

And it caused another phenomenon. A lot of people began to wonder aloud why the traits of alcoholic children applied to them *when there was no alcoholism in their family!* It suggested strongly that a broad array of problems had a common root. In fact, the author gave a laundry list of those problems:

1. Adult children of alcoholics guess at what normal behavior is.
2. Adult children of alcoholics have difficulty following a project through from end to end.
3. Adult children of alcoholics lie when it would be just as easy to tell the truth.
4. Adult children of alcoholics judge themselves without mercy.
5. Adult children of alcoholics have difficulty having fun.
6. Adult children of alcoholics take themselves very seriously.
7. Adult children of alcoholics have difficulty with intimate relationships.
8. Adult children of alcoholics overreact to changes over which they have no control.
9. Adult children of alcoholics constantly seek approval and affirmation.

10. Adult children of alcoholics usually feel that they are different from other people.
11. Adult children of alcoholics are super responsible or super irresponsible.
12. Adult children of alcoholics are extremely loyal, even in the face of evidence that the loyalty is undeserved.
13. Adult children of alcoholics are impulsive. They tend to lock themselves into a course of action without giving serious consideration to alternative behaviors or possible consequences. This impulsivity leads to confusion, self-loathing and loss of control over their environment. In addition, they spend an excessive amount of energy cleaning up the mess.*

It was a short hop from there to another movement in the 80's: ACDP—Adult Children of Dysfunctional Parents. And a short hop from ACDP to the concept of Codependency, as defined in the books *Facing Codependency* (P.M. Melody) and *Codependent No More* (Melody Beatty). These two books revolutionized the understanding and treatment of dysfunctional behavior. They laid out some tenets:

1. You can be an addict and never pick up a drink or do drugs.
2. Your "drug" can be food, sex, gambling, abusive relationships...any number of unhealthy things that cause unmanageability in your life but that you cannot function without.
3. Codependency is at the root of these addictions.
4. Most people suffer from it.
5. If not treated, a codependent will go from addiction to addiction to addiction in a never-ending process—a downward spiral.

Looking at Point #3 above begged the question: If codependency is the root of all addictions, is there a common root to codependency? Because, if there is, and it can be identified, it would give a tremendous insight to treatment. And, yes, there is a common

---

* Reprinted from *Adult Children Of Alcoholics,* Janet Geringer Woititz, Health Communications, Inc., Deerfield Beach, FL, 1983

root to codependency. But before we look at that, let's go back to Point #4 above. Because, sadly, while most people are codependents, they suffer from another disease that keeps them from getting treatment.

THE "I KNOW" DISEASE

I call this secondary illness the I Know disease. Denial. We all *know*. We have intellectual knowledge. But we use it against ourselves. Probably because it's easier than really working on our issues. As an example, I know that certain people are such negative influences in my life. But I still hang around them. I get *agita*—aggravation—hanging around them. But I don't let go. I hang on. It's a terrible relationship. Rotten. It sucks! I know that logically. But I can't let go. Because I'm afraid. I don't know any other kind of relationship. That's the only kind I learned about when I was a kid. The battered spouse is a perfect example.

Another example is the priest who doesn't want to be a priest. I was there. I know how hard that is. I was a priest. I was unhappy. I was a food addict. I was 300 lbs. And miserable. But I always had a smile on my face. It took me years to figure out that I became a priest because that's what others wanted. And still I was afraid to let go, to leave the priesthood.

For the examples above, the Hindus have a story. A traveler is walking down a road and sees another man screaming, his arms wrapped around a tree. The traveler asks, "What's the matter?" And the screamer cries, "The tree has got me! The tree has got me!"

Sometimes the I Know disease "has" us. There are those who face huge, disturbing issues in their lives, but pretend that they just accept them. No bad feelings. No working through. Like, *Nothing's wrong here!* They try, in vain, to intellectualize their emotional pain away. And when that doesn't work, they get depressed. Then they rationalize that they're so depressed because life, in itself, is depressing. It's as though they'd accept *anything* rather than get out of their intellects and deal with their feelings.

I can offer a true story from a company in which I run an Employee Assistance Program. A work crew was on the road, and one of them suddenly had a heart attack and died. When another crew member complained later of stress, the boss told him to shape up, death is part of life, he had to get over it, like everybody else. Sad thing was, everybody else wasn't getting over it. They were at one another's throats over the least little thing for weeks after the death. They just couldn't admit that it was *about the death*. So the one man who admitted the problem got treatment and went back to work. The others fell into the typical pattern: sick leave usage; hard feelings...And who knows how many hangovers on the outside as they tried to drink and drug their grief away?

The I Know disease can kill you.

THE ROOT OF CODEPENDENCY

Codependency doesn't just happen. It develops over a period of time. A *long* period of time. It centralizes around the fact that we have no sense of ourselves as individuals. To understand that, let's look at an acceptable theory of how a healthy individual develops. Healthy in body, mind, and spirit—*where mind includes the emotions*, not just intelligence or thought processes. Those are three fundamental characteristics that we have of ourselves as individuals.

Body. Physical. We are physical creatures with physical needs. We are also emotional creatures. We have feelings. And we have spirit. Spirituality is the actualization of the uniqueness—the awakening of your spirit—that makes you who you are. Distinct from everyone else. It's your *specialness*.

Here's the theory of the healthy individual. But remember, it's just *theory*. We shouldn't get trapped into thinking that it's what was *supposed* to be *for us*. Later we'll balance it with reality. The basic theory is that each of us develops in stages *as an individual*. Then, when you come to your adult stage, you have a clear concept of who you are and what you want. You can choose healthy relationships for yourself. And you are emotionally strong enough to end unhealthy relationships and move on. The stages identified in the theory are:

THE FORMATIVE YEARS: AGES 0-10

We were born totally dependent. Babies are dependent. They have expectations of their family—whatever their family is, biological or otherwise. We have fun with this in my lectures, especially when a baby is present. Babies are not logical. Their expectations are to have their needs met and met *Now!* I'm hungry at 2 AM. Feed me at 2 AM. If you decide not to feed me till 7, guess what? It's gonna be a long night. And those same expectations persist right through childhood.

Between 0-10 I expect and *demand* that my family system meet my needs. Some of these needs have physical aspects, they nurture the body, but basically they are all spiritual, and five of them are fundamental. First I need safety. If you don't feel safe you can't grow. Not really. Your body might grow, but you are not really growing as an individual. Second, I need love—*unconditional* love. No matter who I am. No matter what's happening. No matter if I'm sick. I need my family to love me. *Unconditionally.* Third, I need security. Food, clothing, shelter. These are the basics I need to be able to grow and learn, to expand as a human being. Fourth, I need to learn the basic life skills. And of these, three are most basic: to socialize; to play; to have intimacy. To socialize is to interact, connect, share, be part of other people. A sense of belonging. To play may seem trivial, but in play you become spontaneous, you let your free spirit out.

Intimacy. This is a tough one. Kids know what it is instinctively. But by the time we're adults we think it means sex. When all it really means is being able to share your deepest thoughts and feelings. Honestly. Without fear.

So there are four of the five basic spiritual needs, with the fourth, the life skills, broken down into socialization, play, and intimacy.

The fifth—the last life skill: I need an identity. Who am I? What am I all about? Where do I come from? What is my history? What is my connection to life, to humanity?

A little child has to be taught his or her history. It's important for their growth. And owning your history—all of your history—including everything you've done—good or bad—is essential to your continued growth as an adult.

There is an interesting line about identity in the Hindu spiritual epic, the *Bhagavad Gita*, a dialogue between Krishna—God—and the man Arjuna, an Everyman character. Krishna tells Arjuna about the man who lacks knowledge of himself: "...which lacked, how grows serenity? And, wanting that, whence shall he hope for happiness?"

Identity is critical. If you do not have a clear sense of who you are, you lack serenity. Without serenity you have sadness. When that persists, you develop depression, anxiety, addictions, and all the other aspects of codependency. So you basically enter relationships as "needy," looking for someone or something to give you a sense of wholeness, of fulfillment. This process begins in childhood and continues through the subsequent stages of your life.

THE CRISIS STAGE: AGES 11-14

You can chuckle at how precise these textbooks theories are. They break our lives into neat little numbers. 11-14. Crisis. The theory says that I should have had all of my basic needs met from 0-10, and, if that happened, I can move into this next stage. I'm hitting puberty. My hormones are going nuts and taking my emotions with them. I actually lose my identity for a while. I'm not a kid. I'm not an adult. Should I play with toys or chase the opposite sex? Are my feet too big? I know Santa Claus isn't real. But can I still go out for Halloween? And what about the deeper stuff: drugs, sex, just plain growing up when the world's so scary—wars, the economy...I'm coming out of my child's world now.

I should have someone to guide me along. Someone to talk to. Someone safe. Here's that intimacy again. And the book—the *theory,* remember, not reality—says that the male child should have that with the mother, while the female has it with the father. Why? Because the first love relationship the boy has is with mom, and the first for the girl is dad. Or whoever stands for mom and dad in the family system. And the theory goes that, through these relationships, children will go through the crisis stage, will learn from the parent structure. They will get not only the guidance on all the changes they're experiencing, but also on the concept and rules of intimacy itself.

THE CONFLICT STAGE: AGES 15–20

You can probably say that this is the stage where parents earn sainthood. The Teenage Years. The War Zone. Because at this stage children are supposed to come into conflict with the family system. It's the child's War of Independence. The child should be healthy enough, strong enough, confident enough, to challenge the family's beliefs and values and take from them whatever he or she feels is right for them. Since the child has experienced the family's unconditional love and intimacy, he or she isn't afraid that expressing his or her opinions will be shocking or lead to abandonment.

DEVELOPING INDIVIDUALITY: AGES 21–24

Again, according to the book—and I don't know where they get these precise ages—the rebellion stage leads to the development of the individual. In this stage the child becomes a young adult, with a chosen value system, the confidence to act on it, and a clear sense of who he or she is. And this is the threshold for the final stage of life.

THE STAGE OF COMMITMENT: 25–

Notice there's no number after the 25. This stage is supposed to persist through the remainder of life. People who have passed through all of the other stages can now make real commitments. They know themselves well enough to choose relationships that suit them best. To marry. Not to marry. To have or not to have children. What job to accept, which to reject. Their individual life styles. *Real* commitments. Because these people are *independent*. They know what they want. They go for it. Not for what somebody else wants. They are not approaching relationships on the basis of what they *need,* but of what they can *offer* and what they want to *share.*

That's the end of theory, how people are supposed to develop. You can even forget the ages. But remember the process. Because there is validity to it. Here's the key. I don't care if you're 55, 35, 21, or 91: *You cannot grow or move in your life until you DEVELOP your basic spiritual needs.* Now let's look at what reality is for most of us.

CODEPENDENTS

Most of us *do not have our basic spiritual needs met by our family systems.* Most of us *grew up abused.*

Abused. Physically. Emotionally. It doesn't have to be a major episode or episodes. It doesn't have to be blatant sexual abuse: rape. Or major assault. It doesn't even have to be the chaos of an alcoholic or drug addicted parent. Sometimes you were abused by your parents' best intentions. An example. You're a child. You're father has to work two jobs to make ends meet. But you're a child and you miss him. You cry. You are ignored. Or, worse, you're spanked into silence instead of being hugged and comforted and given an explanation of why dad has to be away so much. You were just taught that your feelings don't count and you will be punished if you express them when other people don't want to hear them. Or another example. Sexual abuse. You're a girl hitting puberty and the only way the male members of your family can handle it is to make fun of your breasts. This is a time when you need intimacy, not ridicule. Especially public ridicule. And it's worse if your father is one of the perpetrators. Instead of learning to take pride in your development, instead of learning intimacy, the chance to talk about what you're feeling, you experience shame. Shame means, basically, that you start thinking, feeling, that there is something wrong with you.

As a result of our abuse, of not having our spiritual needs met, we go into life searching to get them met. We don't have a steady foundation. We're not sure who we are as individuals. We can't handle conflict, because it echoes the terrible internal conflict we grew up with. And we can't handle crises, *personal* crises.

That last one is interesting. As codependents we can function in society, do our jobs. It's just ourselves we can't handle. Inside we are hurting, sometimes falling apart, sometimes even killing ourselves physically. I was a clergyman for over 20 years. I could take care of anybody's problems, any place, any time. I was a prison chaplain for 9 years. I could negotiate a prison riot. But I couldn't negotiate my own life. I was killing myself with an addiction. A food addiction. But I couldn't even face that, let alone manage it. For me—as for so many others—it was way more convenient to run around taking care of everybody else rather than taking care of myself. I can put this another way: I was so out of touch with myself, my own identity, that I did not have an intimate relationship with *myself*. And if you don't have a relationship with yourself, how can you expect to have one with anyone else?

Codependents can manage companies. They manage schools and hospitals. They even manage whole countries. But they can't manage themselves or real relationships with others. They can't face what's going on inside: the unfinished business of childhood and the new business being piled on each day that reflects the old hurt of childhood. Codependents have frozen feelings. They embalm themselves with substances, their "drugs." And they have many drugs of choice, not just alcohol or pharmaceuticals. As I said, food was my personal drug, my addiction.

Codependents also develop survivor techniques. Behavior patterns. There are three that I have observed in my own experience. I personally fit one of the patterns: Caretaker. The other two are Isolator and Fantasizer. Can you be all three? Sure. Typically one will dominate, but we adapt the others, like a chameleon, to get through the different crises of our lives. It's really not that hard for us codependents. We don't know who we are anyway.

THE ISOLATOR

Isolators can be called the Children of Fear and Loneliness. Growing up they experienced fear of abandonment. They got messages from their family systems like, I wish you were never born, You are a burden on the family, You cause all the problems in this family. They typically experienced this emotional abuse, as well as physical abuse. They grow up empty, afraid, and lonely. As adults they will search for the love they never got in their family system. In regard to relationships, isolators are like little terrorists looking for a hostage. The first person who comes along and shows the slightest inclination toward love has to be captured and held by the isolator. They develop their own peculiar forms of codependency, of addictions.

For example, they easily become addicted to institutions. See, if we never had a real family, institutions become good substitutes. Isolators migrate to the mental health industry. As patients. They play a game—probably unknowingly—that I call Rent-a-Parent. Find a therapist. Adopt him or her as a surrogate parent. And don't let the sucker out of your sight. Take your beeper when you go on vacation because I'm going to call. And if I get to the point where I can't function without you, you'll sign me into the hospital. That will be even more like the family I never had. Three meals a day. Constant attention. They'll even take you out to the ball game once in a while.

Another institution isolators love is the military. It's a known fact that abused children make great soldiers. The military gives them a few things they never got at home. Like an identity and a DI—Drill Instructor—to be my surrogate daddy. All of a sudden the isolator goes from being a nobody to a well-defined somebody: a soldier. And no matter how rough the DI is, he's nothing compared to how bad my real daddy made me feel.

Isolators can find a family in the prison system. Why not? It's a crazy place, and isolators are used to crazy family systems.

They also migrate to religious cults. They become workaholics; the company gives them their identity. We're treating a lot of people today who suffer from post-traumatic stress after a layoff or forced retirement. Their jobs had become their identity, gave them a sense of purpose—their *only* sense of purpose. To them, the company has abandoned them, just as their families abandoned them in childhood. And they suffer from major depression—and worse. Like the case of the railroad worker. 51 years on the job. Forced to retire. The man lived for the railroad, probably did more for it than the president of the railroad. So all he could do was return each day to see his old co-workers and walk the tracks when they had to get to work. Until that time he had been healthy. He soon developed cancer and died.

Isolators migrate to another relationship addiction: Love Addiction. We'll cover it in much more detail later, but it's worth touching on now. An example is the girl raised in a large family, say ten children. There was never enough of anything to go around, especially attention from her parents. So she grew up feeling abandoned. And she tried to hold onto every man who came her way afterward. They became her Possessions. Her issue became Control or Ownership. As I said, we'll talk more about this later.

Isolators will also trend toward a particular food addiction: bulimia. Food is used just like drug, to give temporary comfort by altering body chemistry. But isolators are afraid that people will see their drug addictions, or the effect of the addictions, like obesity. So after they gorge they purge: bulimia. Their addiction is kept secret. To preserve their outer image, they hide it, try to avoid it.

Finally, isolators will migrate toward alcohol and prescription drugs. Why? Because these are "acceptable" drugs. Especially the way isolators use them. Isolators are secretive addicts. And functional addicts. They use drinking and prescription drugs as sedatives, a way to numb the pain of a lonely life.

FANTASIZERS

Fantasizers are the Children of Shame. They experience shame in their families in childhood from all sorts of turmoil and insecurity. They begin to deny the reality of the craziness in their families. At the same time, they don't bring anyone home because of the shame they feel about the craziness, and they look for other families to belong to, as though trying to change reality. If anyone asks about their families they try to cover: they lie. And soon they begin believing the lies. They are off in their fantasies.

When they become adults, then, they are susceptible to certain influences. For example, turmoil and craziness are all they know, so they look to duplicate that environment. They get a rush from it. It's a paradox that as much as they are repelled by the shame they felt in their family, they are also attracted to shame because it's the only thing they know. It's almost as if by seeking shame they are caught in a futile game of trying to prove that the shame in their family system wasn't so bad after all. The key word is *futile*.

Fantasizers are targets for the Disease of the Lie: Alcoholism and Drug Abuse. But, unlike isolators, fantasizers are unmanageable addicts. They are also drawn to what are called Power Addictions, and Image Addictions, behavior that gives a sense of power but ultimately results in shame. Shoplifting. Gambling. Compulsive Spending. Sex Addiction. You can get away with them for a while, but eventually they catch up with you. Then you're hit with the shame of unmanageable debts and lies and the exposure of your cover-up behaviors.

But for fantasizers, that's their "normal." We'll talk more about "normals" in the next chapter. Adults tend to seek what was normal for them as children. For the fantasizer that was craziness, turmoil, unmanageability; the lies and fantasies devised to hide all of that; the rush, the high of getting away with the fantasies; and, finally, the shame of discovery. All of these can be wrapped into one word: Anxiety. For the fantasizer, the normal is anxiety.

THE CARETAKER

Caretakers are the Slaves of the World. They're the kids who never really had a childhood, who went from 3 to 33 overnight. Somewhere in their family system they became parents—when they were still kids. You see this in families where one parent died and the other had to go out to work, leaving one of the children in charge. You also see it in families where the parents are immobilized by illness—mental or physical—or by drugs and alcohol.

Caretakers are the kids who came through for the family. The goody-two-shoes. Kids that everybody's proud of, that always do things right. They are the ones who took care of everybody else, who rescued the family, who fixed people. Caretakers grow up to be Control Freaks.

Inside they are full of rage for the childhood they never had, for all the responsibility laid on them as kids. But they don't show it outside. And they don't want anyone to look inside and see it either: *Don't get too close, sucker!* We say that for caretakers everything's fine. **FINE. F**rustrated. **I**nsecure. **N**eurotic. **E**motional.

Caretakers don't know how to play; they never had the opportunity to learn. They can't relax. They over-think. They burn out. They're caught in a dilemma. They hate fixing things, fixing people—but they're addicted to it. They're conditioned to it. It's their normal. Anything else is too uncomfortable. And yet the constant fixing, the incessant responsibility, causes such internal rage.

If isolators are drawn to the mental health industry as patients, caretakers are drawn as workers. They also make good nurses, teachers, mothers, secretaries...They never ask for their worth. They bitch and gripe and complain all day long. They get old before their time and get crotchety and grouchy as they get old. And if isolators are one type of love addict, caretakers are another: Professional Victims. They fall in love with sickies. The sicker the better. Like, *Bring me your sick and your deprived and I will take care of them. The* issue is Control.

Caretakers left untreated even start to decide who is sick and how they're going to be fixed. They stay in relationships long after they're over. They sacrifice for their sick partners. They become martyrs. They play the victim role. Many battered women are caretakers: *You can beat me into the ground but I'm going to stick with you until I fix you!* Sometimes they're the ones who beat their partners into the ground trying to "fix" them.

Caretakers are the toughest people to work with in recovery. They never think they need recovery. How could they when they're so good at taking care of everybody? Even when they see the description of the caretaker, like the one laid out here, they say something like, *Yeah, I know people like that. My uncle. My aunt...*But never them. Not until they get desperate. Really desperate—as in major depression.

Even as addicts, caretakers are "goody-two-shoes." They tend to alcohol, but you never see them drunk in bars. They tend to abuse food in their own way: the fat, jolly person taking care of everyone else while he's destroying himself physically with food. And they use caffeine: cola and coffee, big time—drive, drive, drive. When I was a clergyman I was just like that. I didn't eat food. I inhaled it. I was 300 lbs. I did six or seven of the large bottles of coke every day. The only time I "rested" was to get the energy to go on another tear. My life was simple: *Rev up. Crash. Rev up. Crash.* All with the help of my drugs: food, caffeine, work. The work was as much a drug as the substances. They all had the same effect: numb me, anaesthetize me, block out my true feelings—and what was causing those feelings.

In a "Nutshell"

I'll sum this part of it up by saying that there are all sorts of diseases common to codependents. Some are physical, like those already accepted as stress-related diseases: hypertension, stomach disorders, colitis, bowel problems. And those coming to be accepted as stress-related: arthritis, obesity, cancer. And many, many more. Basically, if you hold your feelings in, they will eat away at you. If you are beaten emotionally, your body will soon show it.

We're going to go into some other maladies common to codependents. These are non-physical. Like procrastination—why we can't finish things we start. And lying—when we don't need to. And a phenomenon I call the "Splain Disease." Codependents are compulsive explainers—even when nobody's asking them to. And again, as with the physical, there are many, many more. What they basically do is undermine us as individuals. They are the manifestations of our "neediness."

But before we move onto those topics, I want to go back to another concept: What Is Your Normal? You see, whatever your "normal" is—no matter how insane—you will seek it in every aspect of your life—especially your relationships.

What Is Normal?

AN INTRODUCTION

Before we actually get into this topic, I'd like to share a few preliminaries. First, as we get deeper into our subjects, I am going to be referring more to recovery, particularly to some techniques taken from the Twelve Step Program. You'll see this as we go along. Second—and I'll repeat this later because it's important—our discussions of our past are not about blame. They're not about getting stuck in the rut of blaming our parents, teachers, peers, whomever. Blame is a stage to go through, to think out, feel, and experience. It's important. It's not to be skimmed over. But it can also be a trap. Third, I'm going to use a lot of my personal experience as examples. Not to blame people in my own past. But to share my perceptions. Right or wrong, they are my perceptions, and those perceptions influenced my development.

Finally, about the question itself: *What Is Normal?* I've run many separate groups for men and women, and in the groups I pose that question. Sometimes it's hard for people to understand what I'm asking. And when they get it, and answer it for themselves, you can get some extreme reactions. Some laugh. Some cry. Many do both.

For example, I explained to one person that I wanted the group to go back to age 0-10. Take any one day and tell me what it was like. What was a normal day? He thought for some time then started laughing, really laughing. You see, normal for him was that he'd wake up and scramble to get to the bathroom before the other six people that lived in his small row house. After he got his turn he'd rush to get dressed. Then breakfast: a donut and tea. Sugar and caffeine. Today we know the effect these things have on us. He was about eight at the time.

After this "breakfast," he was off to school, but it was a bad neighborhood. It was also the time of the baby boom. So he had to pass maybe 500 other kids going to school, and most of them he had to scan as he went along: friend or foe? Would the next one try to bully him or leave him alone? Then school: a nun ruling with an iron hand. Recess: candy—*more sugar*. Lunch: another anxious trip home and back; a cold cut sandwich in between—mostly fat. If he had money, more candy, more sugar. Then the nun again. Then, after school, another anxious walk home. Then dinner and homework: amidst the chaos of six other people crammed into the house; and *You'd better get good marks or else!* Finally, maybe there was some play time with his neighborhood buddies, but there was a lot of "cutting up"—ridicule—in his crowd. The day, of course, ended with sleep—with at least one other person in a small bed. And this was an "uneventful" normal day.

For another guy in one of my groups, an Hispanic, the question brought a sullen response. A normal for him was a father who thought the guy was "too black." This "too black" thing, by the way, was experienced by a lot of people.

The amazing thing is that these two people, adults now, were just starting to realize that their childhood "normal" affected them as adults. In the one case, it created anxiety, which became clinical anxiety and depression. In the other, it created shame, the feeling that "too black" meant that something was fundamentally wrong with the person—*fundamentally,* meaning something that the person had no chance of changing. This had the same ultimate effect on him as suffered by the person in the first case: clinical anxiety and depression. And both of these men, to escape the pain of the anxiety and depression, "self medicated" with their own forms of addiction.

So, **the normals of your past mold your present.**

FAMILY SYSTEMS

Our normals come from our family systems, and we are basically part of five family systems: Family of Origin, Society—our immediate environment, Religion, Peer Group, and the Media.

Our family of origin consists of the people who raised us. It can be parents, step-parents, or other surrogate parents: foster parents, institutions, even friends of the biological family. Society is the immediate environment: neighborhood, region, nationality, culture. For example, I work with a lot of patients from Philadelphia. There are definite separate personalities that come from the different neighborhoods: South Philly, Kensington, West Philadelphia...A running joke is that if you know what neighborhood a person comes from, you know what part of the Jersey shore they go to for vacation. Or police will say that if they know what part of the city an addict comes from, they know what drug is the addiction of choice.

The religious family system is fairly obvious. Different religions impart—insist on—different norms, and as children we have no choice but to accept them. Fourth, the peer group, one of the most powerful systems to influence us. We all want to be accepted. So we try to fit in. Fitting in means doing what everyone else does. Consequently, because of our peer group, we wind up doing things that we really don't want to. Finally, the media. TV, radio, newspapers...The media also has a powerful effect on what we accept as normal.

THE FIVE FAMILY SYSTEMS

Family of Origin
Society
Religion
Peer Group
Media

THE SEEDS OF CODEPENDENCY IN RELATIONSHIPS

The seeds of our codependency were sown by our family systems. They were planted deep inside of us, in our very spirit, when, as children, we tried to find out what normal was so we could fit in, find our own identity. There were a lot of problems with that because, remember, we had five families, each with its own demands, often giving us conflicting and confusing messages. And each sending its messages with the same dire warning: *Don't change the rules!*

So we ran into things like mom and dad not going to church but insisting that we go. Or smoking but insisting that we don't smoke. Or a religion that says not to kill but blesses troops as they march off to war. And often the same church was blessing troops on both sides.

Then we had the differences in generations. A kid growing up in the 40's, like me, had a different set of rules than a kid in the 60's. And to complicate things further there were differences within each of those groups as well. In the 40's you were taught to be patriotic. In the 60's Viet Nam changed much of that. In the 40's if the cops caught a kid with a beer it was a major scandal. In the 60's they were almost relieved when it was only beer, not pot or LSD or something. In my own case, I was an only child in an Italian-American family. I had some interesting rules laid down: *Don't go out and play, you might get hurt. Don't breathe, you might get hurt. Don't function, you might get hurt.* Basically, do what you're told, be the perfect child. I joke about it now, but it's no joke. I grew up trying to live up to that fundamental message. From trying to be the perfect child, I went to trying to be the perfect student, perfect seminarian, perfect priest. I beat the hell out of myself trying to get everything right. I wanted to learn to ride a bike, but that was *verboten*. So I didn't learn until I was fifty-one. In school, we had nuns. And a rule. Actually we had a lot of rules. But the one I use for an example was *Keep your knuckles on the desk*. If you got the answer right, no pain. If you got it wrong, *mucho* pain—stick across the knuckles. What do you think that taught me about learning? And about **relationships with women?** After all, the nuns were one of the primary groups from whom I learned about women.

Or take my relationship with God. I was taught that He was an angry God, a vengeful God, a punishing God. He was a tool to keep you disciplined, to keep you in line with the rules laid down by the person—or institution—defining Him for you. And, yes, God, of course, was a "He," a male figure.

The point is this…If you think back to your normals you will see where a lot of your problems come from. In my lectures I give examples like the ones above, from my own experience, and I give others, to put a face on our "normals" and the confusion they can create. I give the examples to prime the pump, to get you thinking and reflecting on your own normals. Let's just go through a few more general examples. They're common enough. Let's just list some of the things society accepted as normal over the past two or three decades. You'll see for yourself how they've changed.

Women can't perform high-level jobs.

Black athletes aren't as good as whites.

Mixed marriages—mixed by race, religion, or ethnic group—can't work.

Men shouldn't show emotion.

As someone who was brought up Catholic, I can't help thinking of the poor sucker in the 50's who died after eating meat on a Friday. That was a mortal sin then. I imagine this poor soul slipping out of the body, dreading the fact that now he's going to hell because he ate meat. In fact, I wonder if all those souls were let out of hell after the Church changed that rule in the 60's.

In the same vein, I have an exercise for you. Go to the library and dig up some magazines and newspapers from the fifties. Look at the ads and the advice columns. You'll find out that cigarettes are good for you and that all a woman wants is an automatic washing machine. If you find that makes you laugh, the advice columns will put you in fits. The amazing thing there is that some of the same columnists are writing today—and how their opinions have changed! *Changed!*

UNDOING THE ROOTS: CHANGE

I often think of some of the marriage ceremonies I performed when I was a clergyman. Two nineteen year olds standing in front of me pledging to love each other exactly as they did then till the day they died. That was a normal then. Normal for them because that's what they had been taught to think. And normal for me as a clergyman, because basically it was the clergy who were teaching it. I now think that the only way to guarantee that two people stay in love at the same level is to shoot them then and there. Because if they marry at nineteen and live till thirty, I'd have to pray that their love would be in a different dimension, and a different one again in their 40's, and so on.

Why? Because we change. People change. Consequently, our relationships *should* change if they are to remain healthy. Yet as codependents that's one of things we have the hardest time with: change. Remember how it happened. As children we experienced shame, fear, guilt, and a host of other negative feelings that weren't balanced with the positive: open displays of love, intimacy, clear messages of encouragement. For example, the mother that couldn't be there for us because she had to work could have sat down and explained her motives until they sunk in. But that wasn't done then. Then *children were seen but not heard,* and *they wouldn't understand anyway.* Yet even if children don't understand certain words they understand actions. An attempt to explain things would have gone a long way to making the child feel secure.

But again, as codependents, we didn't get the *feeling* of security or other positives. We didn't get them from our primary family or our other families of origin. What we did get were the rules. Follow the rules and you'll be accepted. And the Mother of All Rules: *Don't Change the Rules!*

Now you wonder why you don't like change?

Codependents don't like *any* change. Major or minor.

Have you ever seen a codependent get a divorce? It takes about eighteen years. They know it's over but they won't let go. Why? Because of a lot of things, one of which is a normal they learned a long time ago: *You don't get a divorce! Divorce equals failure!*

But I can go you one better from my own experience. I knew I wanted to leave the priesthood ten years before I actually did. I finally took a leave of absence. And guess what I did? I went out into the world as *Father* Vince and started halfway houses for alcoholics, in effect doing the same kind of "caretaker" work I had done in the parish.

It took a therapist to show me what I was doing, what codependents typically do. He told me I was living with one foot on either side of a picket fence. That's a pretty painful journey, right? But that's what we codependents do. We keep one foot in the past and one in the future, and we hurt like hell in the middle. I have an illustration I use in my lectures. I walk like I'm dragging a ton of weight behind me. Staggering. Groaning. And bitching about it. But that's what we codependents do. The weight we drag is from our past, from our normals. We won't give them up. We won't change.

And it's not only the major changes we fear. It's not just about divorce and career changes. It's about the smaller things, too. It's as though in learning to doubt ourselves on the larger issues we also learned to include the small ones. I closed the first chapter by talking about another codependent malady, similar to the "I Know" disease. I called the second one the "'Splain Disease." But before I go into it I want to go back to another point from my experience in leaving the priesthood.

GEOGRAPHICAL CHANGES

So often codependents substitute geographical change for a real, complete change. I did it when all I did was leave the rectory while taking my religious title and my work-aholism and other addictions—and all the underlying causes of those addictions—with me. So what did I really change? My address? And what good did it do me? Eventually I had to face the fact that I wasn't happy, or *healthy*—and that's a key point that we're going to get to—and that I wouldn't have much of a life until I made a real change. Making that real change meant giving up the I Know disease. It wasn't enough to say, for example, I know my families of origin had their quirks and they affected me, but I should just get over it and get on with it without taking the time to really explore those "quirks" and how they affected me, how they made me *feel*. And how my feelings made me act. And I had to give up the myth of a geographical change being enough to set my life straight, make it healthy.

In my EAP work for companies, I see people who blame the job for their codependency. *If only I had a different job, get away from these a—holes.* But guess what? They get a different job with a different company and their problems don't go away. They go with them. Or take the person who says, *I just need a change of location. If I lived in a quieter place, the seashore or country, my problems would go away.* You think so? The Unabomber lived like a hermit. Did his psychological problems go away?

If you really want to shed your codependency, get used to the facts. You are going to have to identify your issues. You are going to have to feel feelings that you buried long ago—and that can be very painful. You are going to have to *own* your past, hold it and look at it, so you can finally let it go. That is the change that will work, that will enable your relationships to work.

PERMISSION

Permission. I have to inject that phenomenon here. It might sound silly, but psychiatrists, psychologists, and counselors at all levels have noticed something about many of their clients: they feel that they don't have *permission* to change. Remember. The Mother of All Rules: *Don't Change the Rules!* That message was given long ago. And now there's nobody there to take it back, to give permission to change. So we get stuck. Stuck with our old normals.

THE 'SPLAIN DISEASE

We codependents won't even give ourselves permission to make the small changes in life. At the height of my food addiction I was over 300 lbs. Compulsive overeater. Big time. (Big in every sense of the word.) And every year I came up against one of the most powerful normals a human being can face: Tradition. In my family, an Italian family, we had the tradition: *vigile.* Christmas Eve Dinner. In our family sixty-five people would get together—at somebody's house yet—and have *thirteen* different courses of fish—with all the side dishes and trimmings. And you had to eat one of each. Tradition: no choice. After dinner we went to midnight Mass. After Mass—about 1:30 in the morning—we had *breakfast!* Then we slept for a few hours to get ready for the Christmas Day feast, which went from about noon to ten at night.

I was over 300 lbs. I felt miserable as it was. I knew that holiday gorging was poison for me. But how could I break *tradition*? In my mind, I had no choice but to stuff myself.

But far below traditions, and rituals, that challenge us to make choices, we have everyday events. And here's where the 'Splain Disease comes in. Codependents have to explain everything to other people. Somebody asks us to come to a party Friday night. We really don't want to go, but we say uh, um, uh, got to go check and see if I can make it, then maybe even say we'll make it, then Friday comes and we call and say I can't make it because the carburetor in my car went. The truth is the car's fine, but we explain and we lie.

Or ask a codependent to go to a movie when they really don't want to. Instead of just saying they don't want to go, they go into another uh, um, uh, I really would like to go but I have to go here and I have to go there and...Hey, by the time you finish your explanation, I'll miss the movie!

We explain when we don't have to. We explain when no one asks for an explanation. We explain to other people because we're afraid that they won't like us if we say no, if we make an honest choice. And guess what? We explain to ourselves—even when we don't need it. An example. Ever decide to call in sick to work when you're not sick? Say you've been working hard, you need a mental health day, you have plenty of time saved, and nothing really critical is going on in work that day anyway.

I'm telling you, if you live with a codependent who's going to call in sick, get a motel room for the night. They can make TV sitcoms out of this. The codependent will have thirty-three anxiety attacks the night before they have to call because they already feel guilty about it. And between attacks they start getting their story ready. It starts out like a one line message and ends up like a book: explaining again. Rehearsing the explanations they're going to give when they call in, while explaining to themselves that they're entitled to the day off, the story will work, no one will guess that they're really not sick, and on and on. Now, remember. This is all in preparation for a day *off.*

After a sleepless night they make the call. But the guy on the other end maybe just worked the night shift and only wants to get home, so you start your explaining and he cuts you short. He notes that you'll be out sick and cuts the rest short and hangs up. Now you got a major problem. Nobody listened to your story and you're wondering why. So you spend all day polishing the story, getting ready for the next day at work. And this is your day *off. The* next day you finally get to work—exhausted from all the explaining and worrying—and guess what? Nobody knows you were gone. You sign in and go to your work station. But you can't work. You have this great story—even though it's not true—and you have to tell it to somebody. You have to explain why you were out sick just so you can feel better!

And we wonder why our relationships don't work?

It's insanity. Insanity isn't just raving in an asylum some-where. It's the craziness we create in our own lives. The 'Splain Disease is one form of it. If you suffer from it, try something. Try answering somebody without giving an explanation. Just say what you feel and let it go. But I warn you. It's going to be scary. Scary. That's what the child in you will feel. Because giving up insanity creates a very uncomfortable situation. Very uncomfort-able. Sanity. Because the little child inside of you—your past and all its normals—is not used to sanity. That's why people report that the Second Step of the Twelve Step Program—where it says, "...will be restored to sanity..."—becomes so frightening to them. They just aren't used to it.

The other thing to remember about your recovery, the process by which you move from insanity to sanity, is that it is an *ongo-ing* process. We have a saying about it: *Progress, not perfection.* Because your insanity, your codependent patterns, will keep pulling you back. For example, when I was a kid, I was fat, and I was teased about it. Consequently I developed a fear about any-one seeing me without a shirt. I would even wear a shirt when I went swimming. Now today I'm in pretty good shape. I dropped a lot of weight and exercise every day. Yet every once in a while I find myself at the beach putting on a tee shirt because of the old fear of how I look.

That's an idiosyncrasy from my past. Those things linger. What should we do about them in recovery? Very simple: *accept them.*

Real Change: Spiritual Development

As I noted before, this book will often refer to the Twelve Step Program of recovery. But no matter what program you follow—the Steps, traditional counseling, whatever—you are going to find some common denominators in all the forms of treatment. One of the most important is that you are going to have to take a personal inventory. In the Step Program, you would write that inventory and share it with at least one other person. In tradi-tional therapy, the inventory might be verbal, with a psycholo-gist or psychiatrist. The point is that you must look at your past, and *own* it, see how it made you who you are today. With that knowledge of your personal history, you will begin to get a sense of that thing that is so elusive to us codependents: identity.

But the knowledge alone won't be enough. You have to *do something* with it. That's one of the most frustrating parts of traditional therapy and why I like the Twelve Step Program. Clients often complain to therapists that though they've gained a great deal of self-knowledge they don't know what to do with it. It's as though we expect the knowledge alone to release us from our depression and anxiety and other codependent patterns. But it doesn't and we get frustrated. Remember when we talked about the other codependent disease, the I Know disease? So many people walk around depressed and angry but are in total denial about the effect the past had on them. It's as though they're afraid to challenge the normals they were brought up on, afraid to admit that maybe their parents weren't perfect parents—whose are?—or their neighborhoods not perfect neighborhoods. So when you tell them that their past affects them they say *I know, I know* but they're afraid to take it any further. So they start believing that life is supposed to be like the popular bumper sticker: *Life's a bitch and then you die!* Carry that philosophy into your relationships and see what happens when the initial glow of those relationships wear off—no matter who or what those relationships are with. It is no less than insane to live so negatively.

In a good recovery program you will learn how to use your self-knowledge to change. You will learn that you have rights. The right to choose *and change* your own normals. The right to your idiosyncrasies and to that private part of yourself, which is protected by boundaries that you set. And you have the right to serenity and to end things in your life—even if somebody else wants to hang on and not end them. You can choose healthy relationships and let the unhealthy go. Basically you learn a new Mother of All Rules: *You **Can** Change the Rules!*

You'll learn something else, too. When you do change, 25% of the people will not like what you do, 25% will like it, and 50% won't care one way or the other!

So you don't have to be afraid of change. That fear is another of your old normals that you have to get rid of. It is something you were taught.

YOUR GUIDE TO CHANGE: HEALTHY VS. UNHEALTHY

In my lectures I am asked very often—*very* often—how someone can know if they're making the right changes. Remember earlier in this chapter when we emphasized the word "healthy"? That one word is a good, basic guide to choosing what changes you make. Forget talking about things in terms of good and bad or whether something is a "sin" or not. Talk in terms of Healthy vs. Unhealthy. That alone will be enough to make a start toward real spiritual development, real growth.

And if you make a mistake with your changes—we all do—just make another change.

You'll get the hang of it.

At this point in my lecture series I like to go into one of the fun changes most of us need to make. We have to learn how *to play. In* fact, I tell the audience that and ask them to get into the spirit by bringing a stuffed animal to the next lecture. A teddy bear, whatever. And it never fails. I get the *Oh, no! A stuffed animal? I don't have one. Can't get one.* So I tell them to come to the lecture anyway, even if they can't bring one. Because I know how we codependents think. A stuffed animal is silly. Embarrassing. And they'll use the fact that they don't have one to miss the next lecture. Which is why, in my humble opinion, they really need to hear it.

How to Play

THE VALUE OF *HEALTHY* PLAY

I said that in my lecture groups people get nervous when I raise the subject of playing—especially when I ask them to bring a stuffed animal to the next session. I also find the same thing with people I treat in therapy. They think the topic of play itself is silly, or too "light," or just plain unimportant. They especially get nervous when I ask them to bring a stuffed animal with them. Some people actually drop out of the lectures or therapy at that point; it's too embarrassing for an adult to carry a toy in public. But play—*healthy* play—is one of the most important things you can do. Here are a few reasons why:

➤ Playing helps you get in touch with your feelings, especially your *positive* feelings.
➤ Playing helps develop a positive attitude.
➤ Playing helps shatter rigidity.
➤ And playing helps shed your fear of dysfunctionality.

I'll go into each one of these. I'll also give you a few related exercises you can try. And I'll explain why I ask my various groups to approach the subject of play by starting with stuffed animals.

HEALTHY PLAY—CHALLENGE YOUR "DEFAULT SETTING"

First I want to go back to that word used above and mentioned in the last chapter: *Healthy*. Why do I put the emphasis on it? Because codependents generally forgot what they learned in childhood: how to play in a healthy way. I have run many groups for men and women in recovery. And remember, don't get turned off by the word recovery. I'm not just talking about recovery from alcohol or drugs. I'm talking about recovery from codependency in general, from anxiety and depression and all sorts of destructive behaviors.

In my groups, I give an assignment. I ask my groups to take one night off from our regular work and just go out as a group and play. I tell them to have fun, loosen up. Just go do something you would have done when you were, say, ten years old. You'd be surprised how foreign that is to them. Many, if not most, jump right to their codependent patterns, to a definition of play they learned as adults, learned from their various Families of Origin as being "acceptable" for adults: drinking, go-go bar, Chippendales, casino...whatever. It takes a little effort to remember the healthy things: like camping, a movie, lunch, a ball game...

This isn't a rare phenomenon. One of the problems in treating addictions is that we have developed what can be called "Default Settings." Like a computer. These are things we do when we don't give ourselves a clear command to do something else. And our defaults kick in especially when we're under stress. For example, a codependent stressed by a situation at work or home will automatically and strongly turn to his or her particular addictions: alcohol, other drugs, overeating, compulsive spending, gambling, sex...As codependents, we need to learn—or, more accurately, *re*learn—how to lower our stress through healthy play.

GETTING IN TOUCH WITH FEELINGS

I'm going to stress that other point here: getting in touch with *positive* feelings. Remember, recovery is about getting in touch with your feelings, especially those feelings you buried long ago, from age 0 to 10, because they were too painful to face. You've probably heard the term "Inner Child." That's who you're trying to get in touch with, your own Inner Child—you as you were years ago. To do that, as we said, you are going to have to recall your history. In the Twelve Step Program they call that doing your personal inventory. And you have to own that history. Acknowledge it. Accept it. Feel it. *Feel it.*

Don't go past that last point lightly. Yes, you are going to *feel* things that you buried and denied long ago. For example, if you were sexually abused and blocked it out or made excuses for the perpetrator, you are going to go back, look at it, and accept it as something that happened *to you.* And you're going to be angry and depressed and guilty and shamed...

And you're going to recall things that aren't nearly as traumatic as something like sexual abuse—maybe a birthday that someone forgot or even a toy that you didn't get—and that's going to hurt, too. In fact, there's a growing school of thought that even without exceptional trauma in our lives, the small hurts and disappointments alone are enough to erode us psychologically, enough to depress us and make us anxious and give in to our defaults. If we let them.

How do you not let them? By taking your inventory. By going through the things that affected you and putting them into perspective. We call that "processing" the past. When you do that, you will come to the point in the Grieving Process, which we will cover in some depth later, that we call acceptance. That's when the depression and anxiety and other insanity evaporates.

So the beginning of the recovery process is getting in touch with feelings. Healthy play will help with that. Because it is spontaneous. You might see a movie and cry, or laugh. Or see a ball game and cheer. Or go camping and be awe struck by nature. Or go to an amusement park and just yell your head off on the roller coaster. None of that can be planned. And feeling what you feel in those instances is like priming the pump to get your feelings flowing again, or, to use another analogy, grating away the rust that has built up on your feelings.

Better yet, you will be experiencing *positive* feelings. And you're going to have to learn how to do that to soothe some of the pain you're going to experience in doing the inventory of your past—and the pain of today's stresses as well. In plain words, you will need a healthy outlet for stress. Otherwise, you'll keep reverting to your defaults to anaesthetize your pain.

POSITIVE ATTITUDE, RIGIDITY, FEAR OF DYSFUNCTIONALITY

These three points can be covered quickly. They're related closely to what we already discussed. But pay attention to the last one: fear of dysfunctionality.

First, though, Positive Attitude. We'll get into this more later in the book. For now it should be obvious that, as codependents, we generally live with a negative attitude. The more I work with codependents, the more I find that we are oriented to three things: chaos, catastrophe, and fault-finding. We find fault with ourselves as well as others. And even when things are going right, we look over our shoulders waiting for something bad to happen. It's like the line in the movies where the characters are strolling through a forest with no danger in sight, when suddenly one stops and says in fear: "I don't like it. It's too quiet." Why are we like this? Because of the dysfunctionality in our Families of Origin. Those families were chaotic and fault-finding. They taught us to expect the bad, if not the worst. Learning how to play again in a healthy way helps balance the negative outlook. Basically, you learn that having fun is part of life, too. And there's nothing more positive than that.

I think it's the *Talmud* that says that when you die you will be held accountable for every licit pleasure you could have enjoyed but didn't.

As for rigidity, as codependents we are like robots. No mystery here. Our feelings are frozen. Our values are frozen. So how could we be anything but frozen? Learn to play and you *re*learn spontaneity. And you cannot be rigid and spontaneous at the same time.

Last: fear of dysfunctionality. This is sort of a paradox. As codependents we are so dysfunctional. Yet we fear—are sometimes *terrified* by—dysfunctionality. For example, some of us are so afraid of dysfunctionality that we refuse to face the dysfunctionality of our past. In psychology it's called Denial. I've treated people who come in complaining of depression and anxiety, of headaches, of chronic anhedonia—inability to enjoy anything...Some even have marked nervous tics—they actually twitch from stress. Yet when I suggest that they start looking at their past, at their Families of Origin, they refuse, insisting that there was nothing wrong with the way they were brought up. They exhibit the I Know disease: *I know I didn't have the perfect family or perfect friends or perfect environment but nobody does, so my problems can't be coming from there.* And in trying to deny their past dysfunctionality they become married to their present dysfunctionality: the headaches, depression, nervous tics, drinking, overeating, gambling...whatever.

My point here is this: Don't be afraid of dysfunctionality. The entire *world* is dysfunctional. The purpose of it is that you learn from dysfunctionality. So accept it. Accept that part of yourselves. Get into your own recovery. And learn from it. And in the meantime, enjoy life. Play a little.

Just think of what happens to a relationship when what you bring to it is tainted by a negative attitude, rigidity, and fear of dysfunctionality. After the honeymoon wears off, the negative attitude makes you a burden; where's the fun, the joy? Rigidity kills creativity, so how does the relationship stay fresh and spontaneous? And fear of dysfunctionality makes you super critical, so afraid of doing something dysfunctional, something wrong. Ever live with a super-critical person?

TWO STORIES: THE FISHERMAN, STUFFED ANIMALS

There's a little story about a fisherman that I'd like to share with you. He was standing on the bank of a stream, casting, reeling in, casting, reeling...Another fisherman came along and took up the spot next to him. This second man was older and his equipment was top-notch, obviously custom made, very expensive. After a while he struck up a conversation with the first man and was impressed with his intelligence and straightforward manner. The older man asked him what he did for a living and he said he lived in the small town next to the stream. He did odd jobs to support his family. They did OK by that. And he had plenty of time for fishing. The old man responded by telling him that he was CEO of a big corporation, he liked the younger man's style, and would like to hire him as an executive.

"So what would I do?" The young man asked.

The CEO told him, "I'll train you, give you a unit to run, then a division. I'm sure you'll do well with your brains and style. In twenty years or so you'll probably rise to VP. In another ten you'll retire with a fabulous pension. Think of it. Then you can do anything you want. What do you think you'd do with all that money?"

The young man shrugged: "Go fishing a lot. Just like I do now."

◆   ◆   ◆

The second story I'd like to share is true. It's about stuffed animals. I was in the seminary. I don't think you would have liked to know me then. I was very, very, very rigid. Very uptight. Very frustrated. And the God I worshiped reflected that. It was Fire and Brimstone. Good and Evil. Hell. Follow the rules or else!

A lady I knew came to visit me at home one day when I was on summer leave. She said she had a gift for me and gave me a stuffed animal. Now, as a good codependent, I immediately engaged in two conversations at once. To her I said thank you very much, while in the back of my mind I said this lady is crazy, a stuffed animal, what do I need that for? Of course, also as a codependent, I was addicted to pleasing people, so even though I didn't want the animal I was afraid I'd offend her if she ever saw me without it, so I put it on a shelf in my office. And to show you how rigid I was, I took it with me to the several offices I occupied in all the parishes I was later assigned to. I completely ignored it, thought it was stupid, but put it in the same place on the shelves wherever I went.

In 1982, after my mother died, I went through a traumatic week that sent me into therapy. After weeks of working with me on several of my issues, my therapist said to me one day, "Vince, for our session next week, I want you to bring a stuffed animal with you." I looked at the man and said, "You're kidding, right? I mean, you realize I'm paying you for this." He said, "Yes, I know. Bring a stuffed animal next week."

I was back in my office wondering where I was going to get a stuffed animal when I looked up on the shelf. There was that little sucker, still waiting patiently for me after all those years. Somehow, very subtly, that day began a process of positive change in my life. My rigidity started to melt. It took time. A long time. The rigidity hadn't appeared overnight, after all. At first I could only carry my animal in a bag. Even taking it out in front of my therapist was scary, embarrassing.

How that animal changed my life is a long story that I won't go into. Because I'm going to recommend that you get a stuffed animal yourself—or a doll or a pet, but try to start with a stuffed animal—and experience what it does to you.

Silly? Well, let me offer you two things. First, therapists have a lot of success using stuffed animals to work with victims of sexual abuse, especially incest. Second, think of the comic strip, *Calvin & Hobbs.* A little boy and his stuffed animal. It must have touched some kind of nerve because it became one of the most popular ever, with tons of spin-offs: books, calendars...

Why? What is it about a stuffed animal—or a doll or a pet—that strikes a chord with us, gets us laughing and opening up? It has something to do with our earliest days of childhood. Our first toys—or the first toys we wanted but didn't get—were small, cuddly things. And these things to this day touch the psychological phenomenon we now call the Inner Child.

If you are not familiar with the concept of the Inner Child, it's very simple. It is you as a child still living inside yourself. He or she has all the healthy things that ever happened to you—all the pleasant nostalgia. And he or she also has all the unhealthy: neglect; abuse; unresolved anger, fear, and frustration; depression and anxiety...The theory is—and it seems to work—that if you work through the unhealthy—own your history and process it through writing your inventory and discussing it with trusted people—you will nurture the inner you until you heal the unhealthy, settle with it, come to peace with it. Then the healthy, the good, can come bubbling to the surface, to your conscious thought and feeling.

SOME EXERCISES

In my lecture series, at this point, I give my groups some things to do. Some assignments. Good codependents like assignments. They *love* them. Probably because of the structure we're all addicted to. So I'd like to give you, my readers, some assignments, too. Though like my groups you might find them a little different from what you might expect.

First, though, let's make a point: *No recipe ever baked a cake.* In other words, you can read all the books you want, but if you don't practice what you read it won't do you any good. So I want you to make an effort to do these assignments. I'm not going to try to explain how they work. But if you do them I guarantee you two things. First, you will meet another part of yourself, one you've probably kept in the closet. Second, you will definitely experience feelings, both positive and negative. You'll feel things like anxiety and anger—you'll get mad at me because you'll think I'm giving you something stupid to do. But if you do the exercises you'll also feel things like love and trust, and get a few laughs along the way. One thing you'll notice about these assignments is that they concern control. You have to learn how to let go, stop trying to control everything. Because the simple fact is you can't control very much of anything, let alone everything.

First assignment—If you're the type of person who makes their bed every morning and tries to keep everything perfect, I want you to stop that for the next seven days. One week. Leave the bed unmade. Leave the dishes in the sink. Leave the paper laying around after you read it. Whatever. And if you're generally the opposite, the messy type, then for the next seven days make your bed, clean the dishes, tidy your mess. I said try it for one week. Seven days. See if you last *twenty minutes*. See how you feel after just twenty minutes.

Second assignment—If you're the type of person who's always on time for everything, I want you to be late for all your appointments for the next week. And if you're the type who's always late, do the opposite. Now, with this one, aside from watching your own reactions, watch the people around you. Some people aren't going to like it when you're not as predictable as you were. They won't like it when you change—even for a week. I'll tell you two things about this one. First, there's a little principle, a little advice, for people who want to change their circumstances but feel they can't. They're told to change themselves. You see, if you change yourself, your circumstances have to change. Think about it. We are each like a brick in a wall. Shift that brick and the entire wall has to shift. Second, many people in your life—particularly those who like to "push your buttons"—can predict your behavior. So consider the implications of your making a change. Even for one week.

And the third assignment—Over the next week, take at least one hour and do nothing. Nothing. No TV. No radio, newspaper, books, movies. Nothing. Just sit and be. We are so movement-oriented that it might not be easy. I did this once with my seniors in a high school class. I took the seats out of the room one day, and when they showed up for class, I told them to just sit in a circle with the lights out and do nothing for that one period. After five minutes, they were breaking the silence to kid with me about it. After thirty-five, they were getting hostile: *Hey, my parents are paying tuition for me to be here! What are you trying to prove?*

In fact, I had the same kind of reactions when I was put through the same exercise. In college, for a time, we had an all-European faculty. One was a professor from Belgium and I really came to love him, the way he taught. One day he came and there we were, notebooks open, pens in hand. Ready to learn. He asked us what we wanted to do that day. Nobody answered. We thought it was funny, the professor asking us what we wanted to do. He asked again and a third time. Still nobody answered. So he said, *OK, It's a nice day, let's go and have lunch.* About half of us followed him to the cafeteria: *What are you doing? You're supposed to be teaching a class! I'm paying for you to teach me!* But he was teaching us. Teaching us to ask about things we wanted to learn. Teaching us not to just lean on a rigid curriculum and rigid teachers. Teaching us to open up. That experience also taught me just how much we want somebody else to tell us what to do.

But to get back to the assignment...Take an hour this week and do nothing. Get to know yourself.

And I'll give you some other assignments, just as I give my groups. Go do something naughty. Not something to get you arrested or really hurt someone. But something naughty. Get a water pistol and squirt somebody. Pull a prank. I had some women in one group who put a stone in the hub cap of my car. It drove me crazy. It was a great prank. I stopped at two gas stations and nobody could find anything wrong with my car.

Call out sick at work and go to an amusement park. Get some friends together and have a sleep-over. Or just watch TV. I mean, really watch it. Ever see us codependents watch TV? We watch while we do something else: ironing, balancing the check book...Just sit and watch TV for once and get into the show. Enjoy it. Or get a friend and take a walk. Just walk and talk. Who knows? If you really get into it you might just start skipping along the way. Try it. As they say in the Twelve Step Program: Dare To Be Different.

A final note...I can tell you, if you really let go and get into these assignments, you might find yourself doing some crazy things—but *good* crazy things. Things to loosen you up even more. In my own case, I was so oriented to neatness as a kid, I had my clothes separated into good clothes and play clothes. I could never play in my good clothes. I always wondered what it would be like to play in my good clothes. So after doing some of the exercises above, I did one on my own. Got all dressed up. Suit. Tie. Went out in the rain, sat in a mud puddle—and got so into it I actually rolled around in the puddle a little. Now, it's not something to do as a steady diet. But the truth is it felt good to experience it, just that once.

ACCESS THE INNER CHILD

I want to get back to your stuffed animals, because they're a great way to access your Inner Child. Maybe it's because of that primitive chord they strike in us—the first toys we had or wanted. But they really seem to awaken that child in us. In my own case, I went from my first animal to a whole family of animals. I have a bear, Lucky Bear, named after my dog. Lucky is the symbol of my recovery; he rides to my group lectures with me. He reminds me of all the people in my groups, like they're riding with me, and I've had a lot of good conversations with him. We talk about the good and the bad. When I get angry, he listens to me vent. And Lucky took a wife, Fluffy—named after another dog I had—and they had a child, Muffy, and my wife gave me another bear who became my New York Yankee bear. I'm a big Yankee fan and he listens to the games with me as I'm driving. And finally, I have another bear whom somebody left at one of my groups. I adopted him and named him Lonesome Bear because he was abandoned, but now I call him Billy because he's part of the family and I always liked the name Billy, wanted to be named that myself when I was a kid.

Now I'd like you to try a couple of things with your own stuffed animal. The first one's easy. Get an animal, name it, spend a few minutes with it each day, holding it, hugging it, having some fun with it. Look into its eyes. See if the exercise does anything for you. Give it a chance. Try it for a few days. I've seen people in my groups ashamed to carry their animals at first but then become quite comfortable with them. One guy, a fairly straight-laced businessman, actually got to like carrying his animal at work. I remember his secretary calling me one day, telling me she didn't know what I was doing in the sessions, but keep it up, the guy was really changed, happier, more relaxed, and less of a pain to work for; he had always been rigid and miserable. She almost blew me away when she also said that he had bought stuffed animals for the whole staff.

The second exercise with your animal—and don't try this one unless you're ready—is a rebirthing kind of exercise. Take your stuffed animal, lie down on your bed, maybe put some soft music on, darken the room, and curl into a fetal position holding your animal. Slowly close your eyes and imagine yourself in the womb again, the womb of a very caring and gentle mother. Visualize the experience. Slowly, when you're ready, give yourself permission to be born. Slowly straighten your body and sit up. Hold your stuffed animal in your arms as you would a little baby, and in that moment give your animal a new name. Talk to it as you would a little child, saying that you love him or her and that he or she is very special and that you will now take care of him or her. This is an exercise that you can do more than once, maybe at three-month intervals. This is to get you used to the idea of parenting yourself. And if you don't want anybody to know that you're doing this exercise—don't tell them.

One last thing about stuffed animals...If you do start carrying one once in a while, say, to the store or on a walk, watch the reactions you get. Some people will totally deny that you even have an animal. But a surprisingly large number will ask about it and start to get into it with you, maybe telling you about one that they had, or how cute the animal is. Some will even talk to the animal. People in my groups laugh at how uptight they were at first getting used to carrying their animals to the sessions, only to find themselves sharing all these exchanges with strangers when they finally get into it. And, of course, the neatest reactions will be from kids.

PEANUTS

I mentioned that therapists report excellent results using stuffed animals in treating abuse and incest victims. Therapists in general get good results using them as part of treatment for a number of things. They also use pets and dolls and other toys. And I mentioned *Calvin & Hobbs* and how a comic strip can touch us, help us access the Inner Child. There's another comic strip that deserves special mention. I love the clip from it that adorns the walls of so many meeting rooms for Codependents Anonymous. The strip is *Peanuts*. The clip is the one where Lucy holds the football and Charlie Brown tries to kick it. You probably know that this one's repeated every football season. And every season Lucy pulls the ball away and Charlie Brown falls on his duff. But every year—the good codependent, addicted to the relationship—he tries again.

It's no accident that the characters play out these roles. The strip was originally created by a theologian who used the characters as symbols of the different parts of our psyches. There was a psychiatrist who worked out of Atlantic City, New Jersey. I worked with him for years and he taught me so much, God rest his soul. He would use the *Peanuts* comic strip in his therapy with a wide range of patients, teaching them how to use the strip to find out about themselves. I came to focus on four characters: Lucy, Charlie Brown, Linus, and Snoopy.

Lucy is the grouch, the part of us that's always crabby. I call her Lucy the Addict, addicted to looking at life negatively—and laying it on everybody else. Then there's Linus with his security blanket, afraid to let it go, as part of us is afraid to let go of our own dependencies. And there's Charlie Brown, Good Ole Charlie Brown, the epitome of the codependent. Charlie's always trying to kick that football and Lucy always pulls it away. And they tell him, "Charlie, don't you get it? Lucy's always going to pull the football away and you'll pay for it. You're the one who falls down." But Charlie, good codependent that he is, insists that no, some day she will hold it for me, some day she'll come through for me. Some day she will.

Ever go to a codependent's funeral? There's a big sign on the casket: *Some Day*. Some day I'll learn how to play and have fun. Some day I'll take that vacation. Some day I'll drop the unhealthy relationship. Some day I'll do this or I'll do that. Some day. For God's sake, some day is today. You don't know about tomorrow. So do something today, get a new football holder, please.

Which leaves us with Snoopy, a dog. Spell dog backwards and you have God. Snoopy's the Hound from Heaven. The symbol of recovery. He's the free spirit inside each and every one of us. There's a little Snoopy lurking inside every human being in this world. He wants to be set free, to experience different things. For example, he's going to visit Lucy, and the others warn him to watch out, Lucy's in her usual crabby mood. Be careful, Snoopy. And Snoopy goes to her door and knocks and when she comes out what does he do? He kisses her on the nose and detaches with love. Amazing lesson, isn't it? We have to learn to detach with love.

In my groups, I have people who struggle with relationships with their parents, parents who don't understand outward shows of love or intimacy or just giving positive feedback. I remind those people what the Big Book of AA says: *Love Them, Pray for Them, and Let Them Be Who They Are*. That's a little example of detaching with love.

But to finish with Snoopy, what else does he teach us? He tries to take Linus's security blanket, get him to drop his dependencies. And what does Linus do? He gets mad. Just as codependents get mad when we try to drop our own dependencies. And look what Snoopy does to Charlie Brown. Charlie's always trying to control Snoopy, get him organized and obedient. He even sends him to school. But Snoopy's too free. Snoopy just stays Snoopy—spontaneous and flowing and feeling. You can't control recovery. You can't organize the gift of life inside of you. Everything happens in God's time, not ours. What we need to do is open up, be open-minded, sample different things—like the assignments I gave you here. As we cited the slogan before: *Dare To Be Different*. And your own recovery will happen, will evolve.

BALANCE

In this chapter, though we talked a lot about play, what we were really talking about—and I think you know this—is balance. Balance is the real gift of recovery. I often refer to that famous book that puts it in perspective very well: *Everything You Need for Life You Learned In Kindergarten*. The book tells you basically to do your work but don't forget to enjoy, to celebrate, especially the little pleasures in life. So many of us codependents are afraid to relax, are afraid that if we can't control and organize everything we'll never get anything done. But I'll let you in on a little secret. The more you learn to balance work with play, the more work you'll get done. In my own case, I find that by separating the two and giving each its due, I even enjoy the work.

In regard to balance, a friend of mine found a passage from eastern literature, from the *Bhagavad Gita*, that puts it rather nicely, particularly in the last four lines:

> But for earthly needs
> Religion is not his who too much fasts
> Or too much feasts, nor his who sleeps away
> An idle mind, nor his who wears to waste
> His strength in vigils...
> Call that the true piety
> Which most removes earth-aches and ills,
> Where one is moderate
> In eating and in resting and in sport—
> Measured in wish and act—sleeping betimes,
> Waking betimes for duty.

Codependency in Relationships

THE FACE OF CODEPENDENCY

At this point, I'd like to share some true stories with you to put a better face on codependency. I hope this sharing makes it easier for you to recognize it when you see it—especially in your own life. I'd also like you to see how it creates unhealthy relationships—and how you can change that. The first story is a case-study from a couple I actually treated in my clinical practice. The others are shorter references from people I've also treated or met at various stages in my life.

Of course, I protect the confidentiality of all involved; I don't use names and have changed some of the circumstances. And, with the case-study, I diverge from what actually happened in the end to consider various ways the situation could have played out.

As I go through the stories I'm going to use the terms and concepts we discussed before. The more you're exposed to them, the better you'll understand them and be able to work with them.

CODEPENDENCY EQUALS CONTROL

In relationships, codependency manifests itself as control. You see, the great, great majority of us are only comfortable with what is familiar to us, with our *normals*. For example, as we said, our Families of Origin taught us to be shocked by racially mixed, or ethnically mixed, or culturally mixed couples. These couples frightened us. Or, to put it in terms that make our Inner Child tremble, they were *scary*. The same thing with gay couples. And now we have another phenomenon in society. Older people, particularly widows and widowers, are living together without being married. It's an economic phenomenon. In these particular relationships, if the parties marry they'll lose pension benefits or Social Security benefits. They get more money—and they need it to survive—if they stay single. So they live together. Openly. And that would have been unheard of a generation ago. (Ironically, many of those who are living like that now were the ones who were most shocked by the phenomenon of mixed couples when they were younger.)

We are uncomfortable with the unfamiliar. And we are afraid of the uncomfortable—as afraid of that now as we were afraid of the chaos in our families when we were children. Follow the patterns as they developed. In our families, we naturally wanted our basic needs met: security, safety, nurturance, a sense of identity, and intimacy. But our families were codependent, dysfunctional. We were shamed and abused—physically or emotionally—and exposed to all sorts of other insanity, chaos. The chaos terrified us. So we developed our defense mechanisms to cope, to make some sense of the situation or at least give us the illusion of control. Remember, we were only very young children when all this happened. And what were our main defenses? We became Isolators, Fantasizers, or Caretakers.

Those roles were our attempt to control the chaos. And those roles became our normal. So that now, as adults, those are the roles we carry into our relationships. In short, for so many of us in our adult relationships, we look for the normal that was a given in our childhood: chaos, insanity. And we apply the normal we learned—our roles—to try to control it. We do it with our spouses, our parents, our lovers, our children, and our friends. The pattern repeats itself.

And the pattern is usually a two-way street. For example, we say to someone, in effect, *I'll love you if you love me back.* But that's not really love. It's business. An exchange. And what we normally exchange are our needs, the roles we play. Deep inside our consciousness, where we're probably not even aware of it, our Inner Child is saying that if I can play my role I'm in control. So we don't have intimacy in our relationships. We have control. When you grow up in dysfunctionality, you are out of control, so you try to find control wherever you can. It's called survival.

A CASE STUDY

This particular case happened to involve male and female, but it applies just as well to female-female, male-male, child-parent—or to the relationship between a person and an institution. Remember, institutions often substitute for people in relationships.

In the case, we start with a young man. His father was a severe and violent alcoholic. He often beat the son. The father was also a contractor and the son worked for him. The son was almost like the father's slave. The father would also call the son names, tell him he was a bum, was no good, even that he wished the son had never been born. The son did the natural thing; he turned to his mother for help. But the mother was in denial about the father's behavior; pretending it wasn't so bad was probably the only way she could cope with such a bad spouse. So she told the son that what he felt just wasn't true, the father wasn't so bad. See, mommy was just as scared of dad as the son was, so she pretended that none of it was happening, that it wasn't real. That's a common survival technique. In this case it severely confused the son, taught him not to trust his own feelings, as though they just weren't valid or important.

Now remember, this is happening to a child. So he is not only being abused emotionally and physically, he now thinks, in plain words, that maybe he's crazy. Maybe there's something wrong with him, since he's the only one reacting about the father. That's shame—the feeling that there is something fundamentally wrong with you.

The boy grew up to be a lonely young man. So his natural role was Isolator. He was angry, frustrated, afraid, and ashamed. But he still wanted the father's love that we all want, so he tried his best to please his dad—to no avail. In high school, the boy finally found something to take away his emotional pain, to anaesthetize his feelings: alcohol. When he drinks, he doesn't feel anything. But it wears off and he has to repeat the cycle: bad feelings—drink to numb them—alcohol wears off—feelings return—drink to numb them...He was embalming himself.

By the time he left high school, he really didn't like who he was, really didn't think much of himself, really didn't care, in plain words, whether he lived or died. Add that to the fact that he still wanted his dad's attention and approval, and he comes to the conclusion that he knows a way to get it—finally: join the army and volunteer for Viet Nam. Maybe he'll get killed, but so what. He'll come back a hero—dead or alive. And dad will have to pay attention. Finally.

Unfortunately, as he saw it, the army found out he could type. So instead of sending him to Viet Nam they send him to the mid-West as a clerk in boot camp. And somewhere in his mind here's how he sees that: *My dad rejected me. My family rejected me. Everybody rejected me. And now even the army rejects me.* He's not even good enough, worthy enough, to get killed for his country. How does he cope? Alcohol. Embalms himself again.

Now, let's leave him for a while. Let's go to the other half of the story. There's a woman who grew up as the oldest of the eight children in her family. Her mother was so busy having children that she didn't have time to take care of them. She left that to the older daughter. Which gave the daughter her role in life. Miss Goody Two-Shoes. Miss Fantastic. Mother's Little Helper. In short: Caretaker. And caretakers are what can be called professional victims. See, the daughter, as we said before about care-takers, goes straight from 3 to 33, skipping her entire childhood in the process. She works at home taking care of her siblings. She works at school to get good marks. She works so hard she's always tired, always exhausted, and, though she has a smile on her face, she's also always resentful and angry—though she's not totally aware of it. She thinks she's angry from the normal frus-trations that go along with all the jobs she assigns herself. But she's really resentful about her normal, about her caretaker role. It's like that song again: "Yes, I'm the Great Pretender." And when she leaves high school as a young woman she becomes a teacher. But that's certainly no surprise. Her whole life is taking care of kids and that's what teachers do. If she hadn't become a teacher, she probably would have been a nurse in a pediatric ward or some other child caretaker.

Now our hero and heroine come together. You see, once upon a time, they met when he was home on leave. He, still the little child looking for a parent who will pay attention to him. She, the perennial mother. They have a whirlwind fantasy relationship; the fantasy is that they think they are in love when all they're doing is exchanging needs. Within months, they're married. Within six-and-a-half years she has four children; she's basical-ly exchanged one house full of kids for another. In reality she has five children; her husband finally has the "parent" he wanted and will never let go. What they have is a functional—or dys-functional—relationship.

Soon she's chronically exhausted again. But that gives her an excuse to stop having sex with him, which is OK because she's so frustrated and angry and resentful again that she has no appetite for sex with her husband. In fact, the few times he tries to approach her, she does things like clean till three in the morn-ing, hoping he'll fall asleep before she gets to bed. Which, though disappointing to him, is also basically OK, because he has what he really wanted in the relationship: a mother. All he needs to convince himself that this relationship is really OK, really safe for him, is to put a few more tethers on her so she'll never get away: tell her what to wear; watch where she goes; and make sure that, God forbid!, she never talks to any other men. They might steal mommy away. The wife doesn't like it, but she accepts these tethers he puts on her, because by now she is actually afraid of him.

You see, what has developed in this marriage is a mixture of two classic types of dysfunctional relationships. One is a master-slave relationship. The other—since he is really like her child—is what is called an incestuous relationship.

I want to remind you that this is a true case study, a couple that I actually worked with. What happened was that one day when she was about thirty her kids were all finally off to school. Just grade school. And yet she suffered a premature case of empty-nest syndrome. There was no one to take care of during the day. She could no longer use her caretaker role to block out her feelings. And she became depressed. She found herself sitting on the side of the bed in the morning and ruminating, *Is this all there is to life? There's got to be more!* But she was intelligent, so she started to fill the time by reading and following some informative shows on TV and radio. She begins getting a sense of what's making her tick, her motivations. She even starts going to some local meetings and groups—all in secret, of course, because she knows how jealous her husband is. Soon she takes a bold step: therapy. Which she pays for in secret, by siphoning off a little house money here and there. Inevitably she faces a moment of truth. She's learned that her marriage is not a healthy one and she knows that she can't improve things unless she starts by sharing this realization with her husband.

In the actual case study, the wife did share the information. And she got the expected reaction. The husband was very nervous and very upset. What he said in effect was, *I had everything set up perfectly. I work. You take care of the kids. We have each other. Nobody else to interfere. And now you're ruining it!* She was changing. And she wasn't, in his mind, supposed to change.

Up to this point I shared the true story. Now I'd like to diverge and give you some possible outcomes, sort of a composite picture from other real cases that show how things can turn out in these situations.

First, there's the possibility that after he gets over his initial shock he, too, will agree to treatment—maybe only because he's so afraid of losing her. But if they both at least try to keep an open mind in therapy, they'll probably make progress, one step at a time, until they see the unhealthiness in their relationship and work to change that into something healthy. You see, many people are afraid of what they'll find out in therapy about themselves or their relationships. Yet the reality is that many find their problems are very average, if painful to live with and face; that they can be corrected with patient and sincere work—an open mind and effort; and that their depression and anxiety and negative compulsions diminish as the problems are faced. When it comes to relationships, some resist facing their problems because they're afraid to let go of a relationship. *What if I really did marry the wrong person?* The short answer to all of this is that there is a saying common to all good therapies: *Trust the process.* Do your work, whatever it is—counseling, Twelve Step, meditation, prayer...or a combination of these and other types of therapy—and trust the process. *When you are ready* the process will take you to where you are supposed to be.

But to get back to our couple, maybe they work on their problems together and develop a healthy relationship.

But let's say the husband can't face the change. He will try to bring things back to the way they were before. And remember he is an Isolator. If he is a *passive* isolator, he'll begin to pout, then threaten: *If you don't come back to the way things were before I'll hurt myself—maybe even commit suicide.* If he is an *aggressive* isolator, he can become truly insane and dangerous. You've heard the term "Restraining Order." You've heard of all kinds of situations where aggressive isolators have actually killed people rather than let them go—or see them change. That, too, is a possible outcome.

And then there are the kids. They're caught in the middle either way. And being kids they, too, will resent the change, at least at first. And guess who they'll blame? Dad? No. They'll blame mom. She, after all, is the one upsetting the apple cart. You see, she, too, as well as dad, was responsible for creating a fantasy in the kids' mind: *Everything is OK in this family, everything is terrific, and it will never change and dad and I will always be together.* The kids will need their own work to adjust to the change, because mom's change is making them deal with reality now, deal with their own unhealthy "stuff." So basically the kids are scared to death. Scared of what dad will do. They'll walk on eggs around him, taking whatever reaction they get from him just so he doesn't go off the deep end. And scared of the internal changes mom's actions have triggered in them. And they'll let mom know it, blaming her, complaining to her, but guess what? That's also a very healthy reaction because the fact that they communicate with mom shows that they trust her, that they know that, no matter what, she will not abandon them, that they can talk to her.

So there are some possible scenarios. Needless to say, it will take a lot of courage for the woman, as her own person, as a wife, and as a mother, to continue on the path of healthy change, which we call recovery.

CODEPENDENT BLINDNESS

Sometimes when I think of codependent relationships I think of the biblical observation: *They have eyes but do not see.* We don't realize how insane we get—both as perpetrators *and* victims. We can almost understand how a perpetrator can't see his or her own craziness. After all, it's usually clear something has pushed them past reality. But, as codependents, we're often so confused we don't even know when we're being victimized or threatened. Somebody once put it this way: *It's the victims who end up in the depression ward.* Let me give you an example.

A woman called me and said she was going out with a man for six months and couldn't understand his behavior. I asked her to explain and she said, *Well, aside from the times I see him, he leaves me all these messages on my voice mail. I come home and the whole tape is wound out. On top of that he calls me at work all the time. It's almost like he's checking on me or something. You know, I thought we had a nice relationship, but now I'm starting to wonder. He's always saying things like you're mine and I'll never let you go, you'll always be mine.* This man had even gone so far as to tell her that if they ever broke up, he would look for her and find her. And she actually asked me: *Is this normal behavior?* Even when I said NO! she still had doubts, thinking things like, *But maybe there's something I did to upset him, give him a reason to not trust me. Maybe it's my fault.*

Or in another case...A couple came in to see me because the wife didn't understand some of her husband's behavior. I asked for an example, and she told me that he keeps a picture of him and his first wife over their bed. She actually asked if this was strange. When I told her it was more than strange, it was bizarre, she went on to say that he always talks—to *her*—about the first wife. I had to let her in on something. Not only was he sick. She was, too.

In a third case, I worked with a man who had been divorced for *seven years*. His ex was remarried. But he still called her at least once a month to let her know that he was still there, still waiting, when she was ready she could just come back. In his mind, she was just on a lark. She was still his. And guess what? When she came back she'd never get away again. He even went so far as to drive over to her house in a snowstorm, just to plow out her driveway for her. Just like trying to please mommy again—and other sick, unhealthy stuff.

CENTER YOUR LIFE

In all of the above cases—and many you hear about and read about and see on TV—you have one codependent living for another—and sometimes the other just feeding off it. The problem is that codependents do not know how to have healthy relationships. So they migrate into situations like those above and so many more. In my lectures I often ask for two volunteers. First I have them stand with their backs touching. I explain that this is like the isolator/caretaker relationship. They have contact. But they have no intimacy; there is no eye contact or other active "touching." Then I have the volunteers turn, face each other, put their hands on each other's shoulders, and step back so that they are leaning. That represents a general codependent relationship.

If he moves, she's finished, falls flat, and vice versa. It's called "stuck."

The problem is that we think we come together as two halves to make a whole. We think that's how it should be. So romantic! Sorry, but that's just unhealthy. A relationship should be two *whole* people coming together to form something more by their interaction. They add to each other. But they are separate. Along this line, I ask my volunteers to do a third thing. Face each other. Take a step back, maybe two. It represents a healthy relationship. Two separate people. They have eye contact, clarity between them. They can reach out and touch—if they want. It's like the philosopher Khalil Gibran said. Take two pillars of a temple. If they are too far apart, the temple falls down. But, if they are too close, it also falls down.

How do you get to a good relationship? Let me go back to something simple: play. Learn to play. Play is socialization. Learn socialization and you learn healthy intimacy. It's the exact opposite of going out to "pick somebody up"—or get "picked up." It's also the opposite of that other phenomenon: kids going steady in grade school. How did it get so "heavy," so complicated?

Socialization is centuries old and it works. It is also fun. It's like the old-fashioned concept of group dating. Fifteen or twenty people go out to picnic or bowl or play a game or whatever. No deals. No contracts. Nobody belongs to anybody else. Through socialization, some people will migrate into your life and become friends. Some will become significant others. And maybe later one will become your primary relationship. Maybe. When it's supposed to happen. And you can learn to be yourself in the meantime. Like the old Carly Simon lyrics, when her lover is pressing her to marry: *I've never learned to be just me yet, by myself.* Sadly, the lyrics end with her giving in—like a good codependent: *he wants to marry me. We'll marry.*

If you are a whole person, you know something: Nothing else in this world is the center of your life; YOU are the center of your life. Which does not mean that your life itself can't be centered on healthy things. And when I say nothing else is the center of your life, I also mean institutions. When I was a clergyman, we had people trying to live their lives centered on the church. They were there more than I was, and I was the priest! They lived for the church, would die for it—and used it to run away from their families and other problems. Once a bunch of them were sitting in the kitchen in the rectory and complaining about how nobody else in the church did anything, they had to do it all. And I got real brave and told them, God forbid anybody else try to help out, they'd kill them. It's called control. *This is our place, our life. We're in charge.* It comes from emptiness.

You see, if you accept yourself as the center of your life, then you have to work. Work on your issues. Work to make yourself a whole person. Then you learn to give people space and let them have a life of their own. Parents, friends, spouses, acquaintances. They have lives of their own. Even your children. In my practice, I hear complaints like *"My relationship with my kid isn't where I want it. I want my kid to be my best friend."* Guess what? Your kids are not going to be your best friends. They are your children. They can be your friends, but not your best friends. Your best friends will be your peers—people you can share with and interact with on your own level. People who accept—and offer—the bottom line: *I don't have to give up me to be with you.* I can have other friends. You can have yours. Some will be friends we share. I can do things. You can do things. Some things we'll do together. Some we will do on our own. Even if we're married.

That's called giving up control, giving up codependency. You don't need to control anybody else. You don't need to organize them or try to run their lives. Work on yourself. Take care of yourself. If you do that you're saying good-bye to codependency and all the unhealthy things that go with it. In fact, it has been my experience that, if you work on yourself, take care of yourself, *everything else* falls into place.

The Roles That Codependents Play

THE POWER OF ROLES

Back in the first chapter, we talked about the root of code-pendency: *Lack of a sense of identity*. Codependents—*we*—basically go through life with little or no sense of who we really are. We saw how we take on certain roles and how those roles affect us. I started with roles that I commonly observe in my own practice and in my own experience: Isolator, Fantasizer, Caretaker. Now I would like to go deeper into the subject by describing other roles generally accepted as psychological phenomena; in short, roles that are also common to us all. And roles that are not healthy for us.

The main purpose of this book, from the beginning through this chapter, is to help you see who you've become by playing your own various roles—how those roles negatively affect you and, consequently, your relationships, and how strong a hold they have on you. After this chapter I would like to introduce you to a process. It's called the Six Stages of Recovery. The process is something you can *do*—**work** *with*—to convert your own codependency into a healthy lifestyle.

Before I go into an actual description of the roles referred to above, I want to emphasize just how—and *why*—all of our roles have such a strong hold on us. I want to answer the question that I've heard—and asked myself—so many times: *If I know these roles are so unhealthy, why don't I just stop playing them?* There are two basic reasons: Time and Motivation.

First, we adopted—or programmed ourselves into—our roles since childhood. How long ago was that for you? Twenty, thirty, forty years? For some it's even longer. As we said, these roles have become our normal, and change is a very uncomfortable, very scary, thing for us.

Second: Motivation. We adopted our roles for the most powerful reason of all: Survival. And this brings into play two other concepts: Abandonment and Loyalty. I'll go into more detail on these later, but for now here's a brief description of the process. As a child, to be abandoned by our Families of Origin equates to fear of death, nothing less. *If I lose my family, who will take care of me?* To avoid being abandoned, we decide—often on an *unconscious* level—to give our family, our religion, our culture—whatever—our loyalty by playing the role or roles they will accept from me. *If they accept me I won't be abandoned. I will survive.* Remember, we referred to our roles as Survival Techniques.

If you doubt that abandonment by Family of Origin equates to death for a child, talk to some foster parents. One couple I know told me of two separate incidents, one with a little girl and another with a boy they had living with them. In both cases, when the children realized that they would not be returning to their biological family, they began asking questions like, *Do you think when I get bigger I'll be able to cook for myself?* Or *How will I know how to take care of a house? How will I know how to go to work?* What the social workers in these cases explained is that the children were feeling separation anxiety and were really asking *Will I survive?* And the workers told the couple that it is a common phenomenon. That's how powerful an issue abandonment is with children.

I would like to share a case study with you to show just how powerful roles are. Note that in this study the role was played consciously, for only a relatively short period of time, and without the powerful motivations mentioned above behind it. In short, it was a lot weaker than the Survival roles we play. Yet it still had a powerful effect.

A PERSONAL CASE STUDY

When I was a university student, I took a course in speech and drama. As part of the course we were assigned a character that we would play in an actual stage production. We had to start getting into the role—actually living it—for six weeks prior to the production. We had to dress and act like our characters twenty-four hours a day, in class and in our dorms.

Before that assignment, I wondered why they had a psychologist on staff. I didn't think much of it past general curiosity. I got my role: the character Animal from the movie *Stalag 17*. If you've seen the film you remember Animal: dirty long johns; scruffy five-o'clock-shadow; stubby cigar. It was a fun role and I got into it. I did the six weeks before the play and then another six weeks during the production itself, with a show every night, seven days a week. Then I found out what the psychologist was for. I had a hard time becoming Vince again when the assignment was over. I had to be reprogrammed. The whole cast went through the experience. We had become our characters. Or, in another way, our characters had become our normals. And we had a problem changing back.

So now go back to your own experience. You've been playing your codependent roles virtually all your life and for the most powerful of motivations. It's the only "character" you know. It's the only way you functioned. Do we really have to ask why our roles have such a powerful hold on us?

Going back to my own experience, when I was a priest, I knew I wanted to leave the priesthood. But, as a good codependent, it took me *ten years* to finally make the decision. Ten years for me to finally face the questions that evolved during that period from my unconscious to my conscious, that went from being vague thoughts to stark fears: *What will I do? How will I function? What will people think? Where will I go?* And on and on.

Codependency traps us. We become afraid to change. When we think about change, we think things like, *OK, work the whole thing out for me first, give me all the answers, and then I'll make a decision, make the change.* But it doesn't work that way. So we stay loyal to people, places, things, relationships, organizations, and lifestyles that just don't deserve our loyalty. We remain loyal to our roles. And the longer we live our roles, the more they begin to manifest themselves in other ways.

CODEPENDENT ROLES IN RELATIONSHIPS: OPPOSITES ATTRACT

If we live our roles long enough, they manifest themselves in other ways by "growing" into something else, more complex roles. In codependency, there are six of these other roles in particular that we talk about in pairs, or sets. They are: Chemically Dependent/Chief Enabler, Family Hero/Family Scapegoat, and Lost Child/Mascot.

When we talk about the Chemically Dependent we are not just talking about alcohol and drugs. You can become drunk on your emotions, on behaviors, on many things other than drugs or alcohol.

I often call the Chemically Dependent type person the Total Child. The Total *Shame-Based* Child; they do not like who they are—or who they think they are. Their insecurity basically leaves them a mess inside, and to hide that they become, on the outside, very rigid, very judgmental, and very hard on themselves and others. In other words, in many ways, they are like babies. They want what they want when they want it or they're going to make somebody pay. I'm sure you recognize the issue: Control.

As a baby tries to control through its behavior, the Chemically Dependent type also tries to control. They try to manipulate people into being who they want them to be, to play roles. If people do what they want, they feel safe. But only for a brief time. Their shame predominates, basically takes over again, and so they turn to their chemical dependency. In the case of substance abuse dependency, like alcohol and drugs, what the Chemically Dependent type does is use the substance to numb the feeling of shame. Or, as I put it, they *embalm* themselves. Temporarily. Because when the effect of the abused substance wears off, they're back to the cycle: Shame, Chemical Abuse, Embalmment, Shame...

Chemically Dependent types naturally find Enablers, getting closest to what we call the *Chief* Enabler. This could be the spouse of an alcoholic. That spouse is always complaining, always trying to change the other person—but always accepting of the alcoholism in the end. It's as though the Chief Enabler is the consummate Caretaker—addicted to fixing—or to going through the motions of trying to fix—the other, the Chemically Dependent. Like the Chemically Dependent, the Chief Enabler is also very rigid, and, again, the issue is control. Big-Time control. Chief Enablers never play. They never have any fun. They're always analyzing. And so they're very resentful.

Of the two, in fact, as sick as the Chemically Dependent type is, the Enabler is much sicker. At least the Dependent takes a break once in a while and gets drunk, high, or emotional to get some relief. Enablers don't take breaks; they break down—as in nervous breakdown. So both of these types pay a heavy price for trying to control other people.

Second pairing: Family Hero and Family Scapegoat. Their main issue is Attention. Each seeks it in his or her own way. The Hero gets it by always doing what the family wants—never mind what the Hero really wants. They're called the Pedestal Children. They always come through for everybody else, so everybody puts them on a pedestal. We joke that when they die they put statues of the Heroes up in the park. But what happens to statues? Pigeons come and crap on them. And that's the problem for the Hero. They get crapped on. They're never happy, because they're not doing what *they* want. They're some of the loneliest people in the world. And if they wise up and try to shed their role of Hero, guess what? Nobody likes them any more. They fall from grace. The Hero is not allowed to have a life of his or her own.

In my own history, I was *thirteen* when I went into the seminary. I didn't realize it at the time, but I wasn't doing it for me. In my ethnic group, having a priest in the family was a great honor. It was my mother's dream. And so I was living to fulfill her dream. And I did even more: first in the family to graduate college, first to get a Master's Degree. In return, the family placed me on a pedestal. I performed every wedding, every funeral, every baptism, every family function there was. Problem was, it was lonely on the pedestal. Think of it. When you're above everybody else, how can you make contact with them? Real contact? I was very lonely, very unhappy. And when I finally changed and started doing what I wanted...It was as though I had disgraced my Hero status. I often joke that I have to check the obituary column to see if anybody in the family died. They don't call any more.

It also takes quite a while for Heroes to realize what they're doing to themselves. I had one woman approach me once and tell me how angry she was. Her sister had said to her one day that the family didn't worry about anything happening to them, because if it did they knew she'd take care of it. It was an off-the-cuff comment. But it was like the straw that broke the camel's back. The woman finally realized that she was the family Hero. And she didn't like it. She was resentful and angry and sad. And she had been that way for a long time. She had started playing her Hero role *forty-six years* before!

The Scapegoat, on the other hand, gets attention in negative ways. Sometimes they actively get into trouble: drinking, drugs, unwanted pregnancies...Sometimes it's more of a passive thing, like being the sick one or the one who takes the blame when things go wrong. I think of the baseball pitcher Mitch Williams. The "Wild Thing." Hero one day. Scapegoat the next. His unortho- dox style was OK to the team when he was drawing crowds and selling tickets. But when they lost the World Series...It was his fault.

Or take the case of an adolescent I knew when I worked at a drug rehab. Her mother came to see her every day, and one day I couldn't help asking her if she had any other children. She did. Two other daughters. But, as she put it, they were good girls, never got into trouble. When I suggested that maybe she take a break from at least some of her visits and spend some time with the other daughters, she asked why. They didn't need her. Look at the message that mother was sending: *If you want my undi- vided attention, use drugs and go into a rehab.*

Another case...Another adolescent girl, suffering from anorexia and bulimia. Her mother had babied her all her life, did everything for her or with her, never let her grow on her own. Never gave her *permission* to grow up. So what happened? The girl is afraid to grow, afraid to move into the next dimension in her life. And as long as she's anorexic she doesn't have to deal with her body developing the way it should, never has to deal with a period, changing into a woman. It's a perverse—and futile—sometimes fatal—way of trying to stay a little girl.

Maybe the scariest thing about Scapegoats, as with Heroes and the other roles, is that they don't even realize what they're doing. I see it all the time in the mental health community. People become permanent patients. "Sick" has become their nor- mal. They get to go into hospitals regularly, and in the hospitals they get taken care of, get all the warm fuzzies—even taken to the ball game for free once in a while—all the attention they want. Problem is, they have to trade their lives for it.

The next pairing, Lost Child and Mascot, are perhaps the sad- dest cases of all. Their issue is Identity. They didn't get it in their family systems so they look for it someplace else. Anyplace else. The Lost Child type drifts through life basically asking other people to tell him or her who they are. Very sad. And very dan- gerous. They're like walking, talking, living, gullible targets.

Especially targets for movements and cults. They'll become whatever anybody else wants them to be—just so they can fit in somewhere. They are also targets for schemes. They are constantly being scammed. These are the types that buy the Brooklyn Bridge from some hustler. There are a lot of Lost Children out there.

You have seen them and you read about them. When you ask them something like, *What do you want to do tonight?*, you get, *I don't know. Whatever you want to do, I guess.* They'll see what movie you want to see, eat whatever you want to eat, go wherever you want to go. An epitome of a Lost Child is a prostitute. The pimp gives him or her an identity; they do what the pimp wants—at any cost. When Lost Children hit the mental health system, they're actually relieved. Some doctor finally gives them an identity, a label, even though it's only something like *schizophrenic.* On the street, Lost Children latch onto one bunch of people today, a different group tomorrow, and somebody else after that. In short, the Lost Child is a chameleon.

Where the lost Child is a passive type, the Mascot is aggressive. They, too, want to fit in. They, too, want to please. And they're all over you trying to show it. Sometimes they're funny, the constant comedian—until you realize how sad they are. When they join a group, an organization, they stand out; there are six jobs to do, they volunteer for all six. *I'll do it! I'll do it! I'll do it! I want to please you, please everybody, want you to like me!* Sometimes they make good sales people and politicians. But, whatever form they come in, they are tough people to be around. They eventually exhaust you.

Deep down inside, the Mascot is just like the Lost Child. Empty. Sad. Lonely. They have no idea who they are. They come on as though if they run around and do everything for everybody and make everybody happy, then maybe everybody will love them. In relationships, you *hear* them constantly: *Are you mad at me? Are you sure? Are you sure? Do you still love me? Do you still love me? Are you sure? Are you sure? Are you sure?* Sad, but after a while, you feel like swatting them away like a fly. They are so *needy,* so *intense*—and sometimes so *belligerent* when they don't

get the reaction they want—that you just want to avoid them.
You see them coming down the street, you head the other way.
Because the Mascot is relentless and you just can't give them
what they want.

BACK TO THE REFRAIN: *CHANGE!*

The good news for all of us trapped in roles is that we can
shed them. The word—again—is Change. Which is what the Six
Stages of Recovery are all about. But before we can get into
them, we still have to come to grips with a few other things.

First, we have to know, to realize, what we've been doing. Just
keep in mind that knowing alone isn't enough. Don't get trapped
by the I Know disease. Also, keep in mind that when you realize
what role or roles you've been playing, it's usually painful. Very
painful. For example, take an extreme case. Take the prostitute
who realizes just what he or she has done with his or her life up
to that point. Add to that the feeling they'd have when they realize *why* they did what they did: they were Lost Children. That's
not easy to accept. It's not easy for any of us to accept the codependent roles we've been playing. We feel foolish. Silly. Hopeless.
Shamed. Embarrassed. You name it. Some of us feel like giving
up when we realize how sick we've been acting. Which is why we
said before, we have to accept—*embrace*—our personal histories.
Knowledge and Acceptance. But don't get stuck there. Continue
with the process. Trust the process. It's leading you away from
the sickening feelings to the positive feelings of peace and joy. It's
no accident that the New Testament of the Bible has parables
like the Lost Sheep and the Prodigal Son. There's a powerful
message in them.

After you begin accepting your past, explore the issues in
more detail. Let's go back to the two mentioned in this chapter.
Abandonment. Just as when you were a child and you were
afraid—scared almost *to death*, you might say—that your Family
or Families of Origin might leave you or reject you, you are afraid
as an adult that other people might leave you. It's a carryover
from one stage of your life to another. Deep down inside you're
saying to yourself that if you make other people angry, if they

leave you, you will become nobody, have no identity. You are afraid of changing your relationships with others because you do not have a healthy relationship with *yourself.*

And the other issue: Loyalty. To me, it's even bigger than Abandonment. I still have a hard time personally breaking old loyalties. Let me share this a little bit with you. When I talk about my own issues, I still feel disloyal. I love my family. I'm sure they love me. But when I talk about our dysfunctionality— which every family has—I still feel disloyal. If I were giving a lecture and talking about family and one of my family walked in, I would probably freeze: *What will they think? Have I betrayed them?* You see, the old "deal" we made still has a hold on us: *I will be loyal to you so that you will accept me.*

How many examples can I give you? Look at the work force today, legions of older workers laid off after twenty, thirty, forty years of *loyal* service because their companies "downsized." They know what downsized usually means: somebody younger was later hired because they work cheaper and have lighter benefits packages. So the old, loyal workers walk around in a daze. They identified with their companies. They feel abandoned. Like Lost Children.

Or look at relationships in your own experience. How many marriages have you seen that were really over, even though both parties still hung on? Ask them why and what would they say? *He needs me* or *She needs me.* Loyalty.

I have never in all my years met a dumb codependent. If I asked you now to sit down and make a list of all the negative people, places, and things in your life, you could do it with no trouble. You know who and what they are. And even with people and things that are basically positive—spouse, child, job—you could list unhealthy situations and patterns. You know what they are. But, as we said, knowing is not enough. We have to change. We have to start by *learning* how to change. It might help to get started by remembering these few phrases about Loyalty: *Loyal to people who do not deserve my loyalty. Loyal to people who hurt me. Loyal to people who are destructive to me.*

Loyal to people, places, things, institutions, ideas—whatever—
that are unhealthy for me.

APPROACHING THE SIX STAGES

With that as a backdrop, I would like to introduce you to the Six Stages of Recovery. This is just a general description of what they are and what they aren't. I'll give you the formal introduction to them in the next chapter.

First off, I want to tell you that they are not an "event." Not a Magic Bullet. Not a pill. Not something you do once and then you're cured. It's not like when you were a kid and thought of going to the gym, and thought something like, I'll go and get in shape and have this great body and then I can stop. And when you got older you realized it doesn't work that way, that staying in shape is a process. *Recovery is a process.* The process of learning how to change.

There's so much out today about the Inner Child and Family of Origin. So many people approach me and want to do Inner Child work and Family of Origin work. My response is that first learn to do adult work. Develop a healthy adult to deal with the sick Inner Child. Otherwise, you'll probably just start your work and then relapse because you are dealing with things you are not ready to deal with.

Of the Six Stages, the first *four* are for you to work on yourself—your present. Zip. Period. Amen. It's not until Stage Five that you do Family of Origin work, and Stage Six that you confront your Inner Child. Again, notice that...They are Stage Five and Six, not One and Two.

Sometimes in recovery work we use an analogy. Family of Origin work, the fifth Stage, is like surgery. To have surgery, you have to be healthy enough to handle the trauma; you need preparation. The first four Stages are the preparation. After surgery, you have recovery. And that is Stage Six. It is an ongoing process of life, of learning and nurturing and developing the healthy you.

The Six Stages
of Recovery

PREPARING FOR RECOVERY

Before you get into your recovery process, you should prepare yourself to avoid some common pitfalls. I can share some thoughts on these, because, like most people, I experienced them myself in my own recovery. We'll talk about them in more detail later in the book, but for now, briefly:

Don't try to intellectualize the process. As good codependents, we have a tendency to obsess: *How does the process work?* But therapists at all levels have a saying: *Just trust the process. It works.* We say that because we're not exactly sure how it works for each individual—just as we're not sure why certain medications work for different individuals. If you try to work out your recovery in your head, you're probably just going to short-circuit your brain and wind up a little crazier than when you started. With recovery, there seems to be a time when you just have to let the intellect go and get into the process and experience it. In other words, don't try to figure it out. Just do it.

Don't try to organize the process. People are always saying to me, *OK, tell me what to do, tell me what books to read, and I'll go home and work hard and settle it all by midnight.* But recovery is not only a process. It is an *ongoing* process. It lifts you from the depression and anxiety and unmanageability of codependency to higher levels, keeping you growing throughout your lifetime—just as physical exercise helps keep you healthy if you keep doing it. There are no timetables. You're not competing with anybody else. You go at your own pace. And, if you think about it, that's the way it should be, because your issues and your experiences are unique to you. Your recovery will happen at its own time and in its own way. There is a saying about this: *Show up for your own recovery!* You show up by working the process and not worrying about the results.

Many of us worry anyway, especially if we are feeling the pain of depression and anxiety. We want some assurance that the program will work, and the sooner the better. If that's the case with you, all I can say is do your best to minimize the worry; in other words, don't start worrying about your worrying. Concentrate on working the program as much as you can.

Don't get stuck in the Victim Game. As you work on your issues, there's a tendency to start blaming people in your past for what is happening in your life now. That's a phase that you need to experience. You have to come to a lot of painful realizations about other people, as well as yourself. You have to feel the anger and rage and other feelings those realizations release. Fine. But don't get stuck there. Your attitude going into recovery should be that you will face your issues in due time, heal the hurts, and use the experience to improve your life now. In short, you will *learn* from the past, not get trapped in it. That is the point: Learn *from it!*

Don't let your expectations SHAME you. Shame is the feeling that there's something fundamentally wrong with you. It is a major cause of depression, anxiety, addictions, and all sorts of other crazy behavior. In recovery, as you realize things about yourself and other people in your life, especially your family, there is a tendency to approach them or confront them or whatever you want to call it and get them involved in the process. A very simple example...You might realize that one thing that makes you feel bad in the present is that your family did not give open expressions of affection in the past. You might want to take this and run to your family and try to change them, *save* them: *Hey, everybody! Look what I learned! If we only start hugging one another more we won't feel so miserable!* What will probably happen is that they'll look at you like they don't understand a word you're saying. And guess what? They probably don't. Your recovery is *your* trip, not theirs. So you'll walk away feeling frustrated—like there's something wrong with *you*. Again. And that's Shame.

Be careful of relapse into addictions and other crazy behavior. I personally had a food addiction. I arrested it. Then I got into recovery, but I jumped ahead to work I wasn't ready for. I identified family issues and felt all kinds of anger and rage. It was very painful. And I tried to kill the pain with my drug of choice: food. For a while I had to forget confronting issues and re-arrest my food addiction. Only then could I resume my recovery work.

It all goes back to the point that recovery is a process. We often call it a journey. A journey of growth. If you try to scope it out before taking the first step, try to figure out where it's going to take you and why, you'll never get started. If you keep getting stuck at sore spots along the way, you'll delay getting to the pleasant spots. For example, I see people who have experienced an event—maybe a terrible event. And the event becomes their issue and they dwell on it until they become the issue. If you say hello to them, they tell you about their issue. Or you see people trying to find the end-point: no more issues to deal with. Sorry. But you'll still have issues about thirteen days after you're dead. Let the issues be. Recovery is learning from them, learning to live, to celebrate life, and to *enjoy* life. There's an old expression. I don't think it goes far enough. But it will do for now: *What doesn't kill, strengthens.*

THE SIX STAGES

The Six Stages of Recovery are:

1. Self-Knowledge
2. Developing A Support System or Recovery Family
3. Self-Parenting or Family Reconstruction
4. Developing A Positive Attitude
5. Family of Origin Work
6. Inner Child Work

Note that the last two come with the word "Work." They are an ongoing process in which you come to realizations about yourself and then incorporate those realizations into your life. In the Fifth Stage you discover that the foundation, the pattern, for your entire personality was laid in the first ten years of your life. You get to spend the next eighty years or so working on them. In Stage Six you discover the child within you, learn how to nurture it, and learn how to build a very powerful relationship with the two most beautiful parts of you, the Inner Child and your adult self. It's like bringing into balance your emotional side—the child—and your rational side—the adult. You see, there are still issues from your childhood very much active inside of you. They create feelings that are often not logical within the context of your life now. Let me give you an example.

John was born by Caesarean section. His mother almost died on the operating table. As a result, he had to be taken from her, separated from her, in the hospital, so they could work on saving her life. She was in a coma for a while, so he didn't get to see his mom, be held by her, feel her, for maybe the first week of his life.

The adult part of John understands what happened, and there are basically three ways it can respond. The first is denial. He can shrug the whole thing off, as so many people try to do, and insist that something that happened so long ago, in 1940, has nothing to do with his life now.

Second, he can fall victim to the I Know disease. He can say, yes, he knows what happened, and, yes, he believes, as most psychologists now do, that the events in his infancy do have an effect on him as an adult. The danger is that he might stop there. He might say something like, since he knows what happened and know it can have an effect, he simply has to keep reminding himself of that and that alone will be enough to negate the effect. It's similar to when you hear people say things like, *Yeah, we all have trauma in our past. Just get over it.* In other words, if you work it out in your head, that's enough.

The problem is it's not enough. You can't work out your emotions in your head. And what you're dealing with from your infancy is emotional. The Inner Child was wounded. As a baby, it expected to have its mother there for it. She wasn't—regardless of the reason. So the Inner Child feels abandoned and angry about it. Children are like little sponges when it comes to emotions. We absorb feelings and then spend our adult lives living them out. Because John felt abandoned then, he often feels afraid that he'll be abandoned in present relationships. Worse, he often *expects* to be abandoned; that's the pattern he knows from his earliest, most primal, experience. So guess what? John often attracts people in his adult life who abandon him. It's amazing. The mind is amazing.

So my third option in dealing with the facts of my life is that I can identify them and work on them. *Work* on them. Get in touch with the events. Get in touch with the feelings around them. Process the feelings by sharing and writing our histories and other therapies. Basically go over them and through them until they lose their power over us. And please note...We are not negating the power of using our intellect. The first stage of recovery is learning, self-knowledge. It's just that we don't stop there. We don't ask our intellect alone to handle something it's just not equipped for.

TOTAL CHILD/TOTAL ADULT

Without recovery, as we touched on before, our feelings get frozen. Instead of a balance between our Inner Child and present adult we tend to let one or the other take over. It works something like this...

Our past emotions have such a hold on us that we literally become children emotionally. Our life becomes unmanageable because we function on the principle His or Her Majesty the Baby. We demand things: *I want, I want, I want...*We carry this attitude into our relationships: friendships, marriage, work...We look for what we never got as a child. Of course, those around us can't give that to us. So we exhaust them, drive them away, in one form or another. Even if they stay with us bodily, they withdraw in other ways. The basic problem is that, functioning as a child, I have no sense of personal responsibility. I have become the Total Child.

But many of us go to the opposite end—Total Adult. We go to all sorts of extremes to deny our feelings. We try to dominate them with our intellect; we analyze everything. Or we take—in our minds at least—the moral "high ground" on everything. We become cynical. We criticize, look for what's wrong in everything. We try to fix people—even when they don't ask to be fixed. We become responsible to a fault. We are always on duty. We wake up in the morning, we don't yawn and stretch, we start organizing stuff. In our heads. You see, we are so ashamed and so afraid of our emotions, our past, that we try to bury them. We try to disown our Inner Child by becoming the Total Adult. Which is impossible.

WORKING THE FIRST STAGE

Notice that we describe codependents as people with frozen feelings. I laugh when I read the quote in one codependency book, to the effect that a codependent's feelings are so frozen they have freezer burn. We have a phrase for it: *Froze from the nose to the toes.* Notice we don't mention the head. Our head, our intellect, doesn't freeze, so that's where we start in Stage One.

Notice, too, that while becoming the Total Adult—too wrapped up in the intellect—creates all sorts of insanity, unmanageability in our lives, Stage One is a place to be skeptical—in fact, to develop a healthy skepticism. We accept the fact that we are afraid. That we do not trust, because we have been hurt. We have put people—and doctrines and organizations and other things—

up on pedestals, and they didn't live up to their billing. They did not cure our unmanageability. They did not make us feel better, feel healthy. They did not bring us peace. So now—hopefully—we have a *Prove it!* attitude. That's part of the learning process in Stage One. We question this program. Good. Because then you can really see what the program does for you. You don't have to take anybody else's word for it and pretend to be feeling something that you are not.

Also in Stage One, you are not being asked to do anything but listen, observe, and learn in any way you can. You don't have to stand up in a group and start talking. You don't have to do anything you are not comfortable with. If part of this stage for you is going to Twelve Step lectures or Adult Children or other groups, nobody even asks your name. That is important for codependents because it gives us a sense of control. We have been out of control so often that it's scary. So in Stage One you control your own participation.

But what does Stage One look like? How do you do it? How long does it take? To answer the last first, it takes as long as you need. As for what it looks like, it might involve you just reading; there are tons of books available at lectures. You might want to attend lectures or groups: Twelve Step, Adult Children of Alcoholics, Codependents Anonymous...There are also tons of groups. You might want to enter therapy. You might want to meditate. You might want to do all of these and more. But please remember that we suggest some group work—attending groups and listening—because you will want to build a support system as you go along. You will want to network at some point with people you trust—and like.

Let me flesh some of this out for you. Years ago, I used to run groups for alcoholics and addicts. It was simple. I'd go in and share stuff with them. They'd sit and listen and then open up with me and the group. They didn't even ask my name. Today the same type of group is more skeptical. They want to know who I am, where did I go to school, how do I know all this stuff, what's my history, what kind of shorts I wear...In short they are challenging me: *Prove it!* And that is healthy.

Also today, many, many people go to a group—a general group—we're not just talking about substance rehab here, but general lecture groups as well—and they hear the information and they start saying things to themselves like, *Hey! He's talking about* MY *mother*...Or father or brother or husband or child or whatever. They realize that we've all had similar experiences, similar trauma. Our issues are similar. We are not alone. And they get to talking to other people after the lectures. They begin socializing in a very safe, very discreet manner. In fact, many of them get into the process more over a cup of coffee with a new-found friend than they do in the lectures themselves. To put it another way, you hear things about others and eventually get around to yourself.

A couple of other very basic principles about Stage One and recovery in general...Do not, do not, do not, do not trust your life to another human being unless you feel totally safe, totally comfortable with that person. Do not, do not, do not, do not put anybody up on a pedestal. Including therapists. They are not gods. Last time I checked there was only one God, as I see it. Therapists are just human beings like you: on their own journey, doing their own searching and learning. If you don't think one is helping you, find another. If they can't handle that, shame on them.

In Stage One you work on yourself and you grow. The process works automatically. So get all the information you need, take your time, find things out, ask questions...But remember: do it on a safe level.

Stage Two

This is where you start to make a transition from your first stage. In other words, you continue doing much of the same work, but on a different level, in a different way. For example, you learn to let go of control a bit. This does not mean that you give up your *safety*. It means that you start to connect with a support group, what we call the Recovery Family, so that you can start to share and process your own work. Who will be in the group? That depends on you, on who you feel comfortable with.

You network. You connect with other people who are going through the same process with you. Why? It's a very basic principle: *You are not an island, not alone.* The minute you left your mother's womb you became part of a family, some Family or Families of Origin. In Stage Two you are going to connect with a *healthy* family—healthy in the sense that it will be open to let you grow—and will depend on you as well to help others in the family grow. *Safely.*

You will also learn something extremely important by connecting with a Recovery Family. When you interact—both listen to others' stories and issues and experiences and share yours— you will learn that you are not the Eighth Wonder of the World or something, not unique in your trauma and your issues, not crazy. You will gain PERSPECTIVE.

For example...In a group, a woman sits, depressed and anxious. She has a terrible secret. Finally one day she shares it: Incest. And guess what? Her sharing—with all the tears and fears that go with it—prompt others in the group to open up and confess their own secret: Incest. It's an all-too-common occurrence. You've heard people say, with all the publicity on sexual abuse now, that the problem was there all along and more widespread than anyone thought. And the same applies to the other issues as well: *You are not alone!*

But you will never know that, never *experience* that, if you isolate yourself.

Can you also do one-on-one therapy? Yes. But this particular program involves more than that. The key to the second stage of recovery is building a Recovery *Family*, a network, so group work at some point is crucial to it.

THE PITFALLS

For us codependents, there are two major pitfalls to individual therapy. First, we are, by our codependent nature, or conditioning, extremely manipulative. And we're good at it. So we'll try to take the therapist hostage. Mold him or her into what *we*

want them to be. I get a kick out of that. People are always coming up to me and saying that they're going into individual counseling—so what books should they buy for the therapist so he
can focus on their codependent issues? *Argh!* You're going to buy
the books for them, retrain them, and pay them, so they can work
on your issues. Last time I checked it was the other way around.
The therapist paid for his own training. And he or she guided the
therapy. Without getting too much into it, I think you can see
where this pitfall is counterproductive. Worse, it can be a form of
denial, delay.

The other pitfall is that we'll do the therapy and get all this
information and then…What? What will we do with it? In my
own experience, I read a book on Adult Children of Alcoholics,
realized that a lot of it pertained to me and the way I was
brought up, and then ran back to my family with the book under
my arm to share my realization with them: *Look what I found
out! Our family is dysfunctional! We are a disaster! But there's a
way out!* Guess what? That experience was a disaster. They
wanted to have me committed to a state hospital!

The dynamics of that second pitfall are simple, basic. I'm
doing what every child tries to do. I want my family to understand. I want them to come on board. I want them to give me all
the emotional things I never got from them. In other words, I am
repeating the dysfunctionality of my childhood. I am going to the
wrong places to get what I need for the growth in my life.

Can I make it a little plainer? There was a man in one of my
groups. He had crashed, been admitted to the hospital for
depression. He got out and went into individual therapy. He
learned a lot about what had put him in the hospital, the issues
that had brought his depression on. Some of those issues had to
do with two very close friends he had known since high school.
So close, in fact, they had often been called the Three
Musketeers—you saw one, you saw the other two. He realized
there was a lot of emotion unresolved among them. Old hurts.
Disappointments. One of the disappointments even had to do
with the way they had handled his breakdown; they had basically denied he was hurting, right up until the time he went into

the hospital. Well, he took his new-found knowledge and ran to them to share it. He believed it would help their relationship, bring them closer. Guess what?

You see, his issues were really his, not theirs. And even if they had agreed on the issues, they weren't ready to face them. Plain and simple.

As a child, I don't have much choice about my family or who I hang around with. I'm born or sent into an environment, like school, where some sort of relationships will naturally develop. But as an adult I can choose my surrogate Families of Origin. In recovery, I can include people in those families who are on the same road I am.

FAKE IT UNTIL YOU MAKE IT

I like the "Fake it" phrase. It's my advice for that crucial part of Stage Two: networking. Group work. You'll resist it for a number of reasons—some of them even valid. It's natural to say things to yourself like, *I don't want to get involved with a group of nuts. How do I know I'll have anything in common with a particular group? What goes on in these meetings? If they relate to Adult Children and other works on addictions, aren't they just for drunks and addicts?* And so on.

But the people in the groups are just like you. And me. People in therapy are just like you and me. Do you know, for example, that psychologists and psychiatrists do their own therapy regularly? They have their own therapists, own groups. And the typical people in any group will be just like you—fed up with the depression and anxiety and other craziness in their lives. Wanting something better. Willing to work for it.

And the groups aren't just for substance abusers. I would like to make that clear. So often people hear me borrow from AA or Twelve Steps or Adult Children of Alcoholics and they turn off. All I am borrowing is the knowledge that these sources provide through their own hard efforts. I am not borrowing their classifications, their particular issues.

Our fear of group work has to do with that little stubborn part of us that doesn't want to let go of control, doesn't really want to take a risk, take *the leap*. Remember a very, very, very, very important thing: Codependent groups *are not CONFRONTATIONAL*. You are not expected to start pouring out your heart or challenge anyone or be challenged. Yes, you will experience dynamics. But you do it *SAFELY*.

I remember once being invited to speak at a group meeting. I was minding my own business, telling my own story, stuff that happened to me in my life, and I got around to my mother. All of a sudden this lady gets up and starts yelling at me. I won't get into her language, but basically she was saying that she hated her mother, always would hate her, wasn't interested in healing any relationship with her, and would hate her till the day she died. Now here I was, a codependent with a particular issue of fear of angry women. Truth was, I was shaking. And the woman ended and just sat down and the whole room was quiet, just staring. I really didn't know what to do, so I just sort of said, well, thank you for sharing. And went on with my talk.

I remember in another group a particular person would get up every week and share a story...It got to the point where, when she was just a sentence or two into it, everybody in the room could have finished the story, we had heard it so often. But we listened, week after week. For some reason, it was important for her to repeat it, and the group provided an ear.

In groups, you take people where they are. Just as they take you where you are. Some say things to test the group: *Will they really accept me after this?* Some are just stuck on particular points trying to work them out, trying to process them. It's not for anyone in the group to decide when the process is finished for anyone else.

Dynamics. You might just sit and listen. You might be prompted to share, slowly at first. You might sit there for a while wondering what good it's doing you. Which is why we say stick with it for a while, give it a chance, *Fake it...*

To go back to the beginning of this chapter, don't try to organize it or figure it out. Just show up for your own recovery, make the investment, and observe. Connecting with other people works. It might work on the principle something like, *Wherever two or more of you are gathered...* Who knows? But it seems that when you connect with people working toward the same goal, something good happens.

It's just like deciding to go to a gym to work out. You're not happy with how you look, how you feel. You wonder what it's like to be in good shape. Maybe you read about it, get interested. Then you try a gym. You don't like one—too much spandex or too much macho talk—you try another and maybe another. Finally you connect where you're comfortable. It gets to be fun.

What you don't do is run to the bar where your old buddies who aren't interested are guzzling their beers and start expounding the benefits of working out. And you don't pick an instructor who's giving you a hernia by shouting at you to add more weight to your workout while you're already straining. It's the same in recovery. Nobody is in charge of you. You get around people who are just like you. Again, you discover that you're not crazy, not the Eighth Wonder of the World of Emotional Wrecks. You discover that—much as we codependents like to be classified—it gives us a sense of identity—we don't need classifications—other than that you are a human. Everything else—all your issues—can be dealt with.

Let me cap it this way: *FEELING SAFE IS ONE OF THE MOST IMPORTANT PARTS OF RECOVERY.* Go at your own pace to wherever your heart leads you. But give it an honest shot.

AN ASSIGNMENT: YOUR FANTASY FAMILY

In the next chapter, we'll continue with the stages of recovery. As a prelude, I want to give you an assignment. I want you to start getting out of your head and into your gut. Before going to the next chapter, sit down and think about what you would have liked your family to be from the time you were born till you were ten years old. Write out this description of your Fantasy Family.

I don't care if you can write well. We're not interested in grammar here. Write it out so you can understand it. And it's a fantasy. Anything you want. Maybe you had no biological family that you knew. That's OK. Create one. Maybe you never had brothers and sisters but wanted some. Good. Create them. Describe them. Tell what you'd do with them. Maybe your dad was a laborer and you wanted him to be a doctor, or vice-versa. Make it any way you want. That's the only rule: *Make it any way you want.*

Now, as good codependents, you're saying, that's silly. I promise I'll give you a good reason for it. A reason approved by traditional therapy, if that makes you feel better. I'll give you the reason at the beginning of the next chapter. I promise.

(Now, also as good codependents, a bunch of you will immediately turn to the next chapter to judge whether or not it's really worth it. That's OK. And, yes, you can read the next chapter even if you don't do the assignment.)

Stage Three: Self-Parenting

MEETING YOUR OWN NEEDS

Why did I tell you to write about your Fantasy Family? Because it will show you your wish list, straight from your own heart. The roots of our codependency are in the dysfunctionality of our Family of Origin, especially as that family related to us in the first ten years of our lives. So when we recreate that family as a Fantasy Family, we are really identifying what we wanted from that family but didn't get. Since we didn't get it, it is still a need. So we are really making a list of our unfulfilled needs. In regard to relationships, we often sabotage them by unreasonably expecting them to fulfill these needs. As we go through this chapter, I will give you examples of such needs, and we are going to do something very important in recovery based on that list.

Also, getting into fantasy gets us out of our heads and into our guts, into our *feelings*. We resist that for a number of reasons, which we already discussed. But let's list some again as reminders. We are afraid to get out of our heads and into our guts because:

> ➤ Our head is our Control Tower and we are afraid to let go of control.
> ➤ Our feelings are too painful to face.
> ➤ We are just not used to dealing with feelings, we have blocked them and denied them and shut them out for so long; in fact, some of us wouldn't know a genuine feeling if we tripped over one.
> ➤ We are afraid of the unknown; we have some very strong hints that we have pent-up bad feelings, but we're just not sure how big and ugly these "demons" are.

But getting into our feelings tells us what we want, what we need, what we have needed for a long time. Then we can work toward getting those needs met. Getting them met is called Parenting. The process of Stage Three is called Self-Parenting; *we* will get our *own* needs met. In short, we will begin to take responsibility for our own lives. We will stop frustrating ourselves and stop carrying unrealistic expectations into our relationships.

FAILURE TO TAKE RESPONSIBILITY: THE CONSEQUENCES

We already know the consequences of abdicating our responsibility to get our own needs met: Codependency, along with the depression and anxiety and other insanity that goes with it. Keep one basic principle in mind: *To get your needs met, look inside of yourself.*

We have a very, very, very hard time understanding that. When we are children, we have friends, and we think, *If only they would do this, or do that, or treat me this way, I would be happy.* Then we become teenagers and think, *If only I had a boyfriend or girlfriend, I would be happy.* And it goes on through the stages of our lives. *If only I had someone to marry...If only I had kids...If only I had a better job...If only I had more money...If* only I had...If only I had...And we get things and they don't make us happy, don't cure our addictions or our depressions. So we think, *Well, if only I really had it made, like a famous actress or ball player or business mogul or...*Yet we hear the stories of actresses and ball players and moguls all the time; money, fame, and all the other external things just don't make them happy. AND WE STILL DON'T GET IT! We keep looking *outside of* ourselves.

More often than not, we keep turning to other people. We are looking to be *parented*, to have our needs met. And when they do not meet our needs we feel shamed—like there's something wrong with us. And we start feeling sorry for ourselves. And we get angry at them. And while we're beating them up we also beat ourselves up. Soon our bad feelings overshadow everything else. We have just enough energy to get up each morning, go to work, come home, eat, go to bed, and start it over again the next morning. That is, of course, unless your bad feelings turn into clinical depression and you get dysfunctional for a while until you can be medicated or hospitalized back to functionality.

It reminds me of that bumper sticker: LIFE'S A BITCH AND THEN YOU DIE! Wonderful, isn't it? You function, you survive, and then you die. And you wonder why you're depressed? And guess what? There's a bonus. You get to pass the pattern on to your kids. They see the way you live. We have that phrase, *I'm coping.* Your kids see how you cope. That's how they'll try to cope. It's a shame. We're all coping. When we should be living.

That's what happens when you don't get your needs met.

STAGE THREE, STEP ONE; SOME EXAMPLES

Writing out your fantasy family is like Step One of the third stage of recovery. Let me give you some examples.

In one of my groups I recommended the same exercise. I got a call from one of the members, a woman. "I don't believe this," she said. "I started the assignment and I'm sitting here crying like a baby." I said, "Congratulations!" She said, "But I don't like it. I have all this sadness coming up." What was she learning? That she had feelings she had hidden. That she wasn't used to dealing with feelings. I advised her to just continue, go with the process. That's how you get the feelings up and out. That's how you find out what you wanted and never got.

In my own experience, when I started reconstructing my mother in my fantasy family, I was totally amazed at what came up. My real mother, in her own loving way, tried to protect me. But she smothered me. She *over*protected me, which I'll get into a little more later. When I reconstructed her, I found myself wanting a mother who would give me space and distance. She would be quiet and gentle, she would teach me and be there for me. But she would also give me the right to make some mistakes and learn from those mistakes.

I also realized that in the environment I was brought up in, women were the movers and shakers, the vocal ones, the active ones, so much so that today, when a woman raises her voice, the old stuff comes back and I get uptight. So I realized another need. I wanted a quiet woman in my life.

Also in reconstructing my fantasy family, I had to look at where I wanted that family to live. My real family lived in South Camden. A tight neighborhood. Everybody knew everybody else's business. And everybody was friendly, to the point of walking into one another's houses with hardly a knock. So I realized I wanted privacy. I wanted a quiet environment.

Now take this to the next step. What do I do with all this knowledge? I choose, *in my present life*, to meet those needs. I avoid people who are loud and obnoxious; I stay away from people who bulldoze me. And I live in a place where my family and I have friendly neighbors—but also have our privacy.

These are choices I make to have my needs met. *Self-Parenting.* Setting boundaries.

So what was the end result of all that dysfunctionality in my early life? It became my teacher.

By practicing the Six Stages of Recovery, *my dysfunctionality became my teacher. THAT'S ALL THAT DYSFUNCTIONALITY IS: YOUR TEACHER.*

SURROGATES

But let's go further still. In my real childhood I wanted my father to take time to play with me. Especially to play baseball. To have a catch, take me to a game, even take me to Cooperstown, to the Hall of Fame. But my father was an immigrant. He didn't know anything about baseball and wasn't much interested at that stage in his life. It was something, quite literally, that was foreign to him. Plus, he worked long days on the railroad and was a lot like our neighbors; he liked to circulate and get into other people's business, actually always trying to help where he could. He carried the humorous but respectful title, Mayor of South Camden. But that meant that he wasn't home, wasn't available to me. Consequently, I never really bonded with him. In fact, when I first started in recovery and they did psychological testing on me, I scored very highly on the female side and very low on the male.

Doing my fantasy family, and thinking about all this, I also realized some other things. I had carried my childhood experience into my adult life. I didn't really bond with other men— unless it had something to do with business. I couldn't, for example, just go out and have a cup of coffee with a friend and talk about sports, the weather, whatever. I'd have to talk about work or some theories or something. I had to be intellectual. I was intellectualizing my life. Living inside my head. Instead of just having fun. Instead of just playing once in a while.

Now, knowing all that, I had a choice. I could continue that way, in semi-isolation and disappointment. Or I could change it. So once I got comfortable in one of the groups I attended, I asked one of the guys to be my surrogate dad. Which means what? Which means we played catch, went to some games, even went to Cooperstown for three days. And here we are years later adding to the relationship. Every baseball season we make the rounds of various ball parks, especially the minor leagues. In winter, no baseball, we play basketball. I'm even ref in the Little League. I am getting my needs met. *By asking.*

And I have other surrogates in my life. And I have news for you. So do you. If you ever had the thought, as most of us do, that someone was like a brother to you, or a sister, or a mom or dad, guess what? In some way they were your surrogates. In some way they were meeting needs you never had met. All you had to do to formalize the process was to ask them to be your surrogate—which they were already doing to a point anyway.

For me, my other surrogates are the nine or so brothers and sisters I never had. I was an only child. When I did my fantasy family, I found out I wanted siblings. Lots of siblings. How did I get them? I basically connected with people, many in groups I attended, and now have close friendships. There are enough of us to choose up games of ball, take trips together, go out for dinner, whatever.

And I also have the privilege of playing surrogate. There was a woman in recovery with whom I became friends. She called one day and wanted to ask a favor, basically to be her surrogate dad for her wedding. Her father was a violent alcoholic still in his active addiction. She hadn't seen him for fifteen years. She knew where he was and could invite him to the wedding, but she also knew that he would show up drunk or get drunk at the reception. She chose not to risk that. She wanted her reception to be a healthy, positive experience. So I was her surrogate dad for the day. I gave her away, danced with her to Daddy's Little Girl, and escorted her mother for the day.

My friend had chosen to self-parent herself, to get her needs met by asking for a surrogate. Some of you might think, well, she could have asked her real dad, asked him not to drink that day. AARGH!!! You're talking about an alcoholic in his active addiction. It's pretty much insane to think that he'd show up sober or stay sober at a wedding. We have a right to let go of insanity and have our needs met in a healthier way.

ASK FOR AND DO WHAT YOU WANT

Aside from using surrogates, just plain ask for what you want from people and do what you want—take your own action—to get your needs met. We find that so difficult. A few years back, I received a call about a friend of mine, someone I had grown up with and gone to the seminary with. He was the same age as me, fifty-four. He was dying of cancer and wanted me to come and talk to him. We talked for a few hours. He was very near death. And guess what he was worried about? He was wondering, basically, if God was happy with him or was going to beat up on him after he died. He wanted my opinion, so I told him. I said I thought we'd done a pretty good job of beating up on ourselves already, there wasn't much left for God to do. In fact, in my opinion, God doesn't want us to beat up on ourselves. I told my friend I thought everything would be fine.

And guess what? That satisfied him. There he was. Fifty-four. Dying. And it's like he needed permission from somebody else to die peacefully. Just as so many of us look to others to give us permission to *live* peacefully. Give *yourself* permission.

I also told my friend that day that I'd make a deal with him, which he did. I basically said, *Look, when you cross over put in a requisition to be my guardian angel in recovery.* And now many times I think of him that way, helping me continue recovery, continue my personal growth. It was a moving experience for me to talk to him like that. First, it reminded me how my Higher Power—as *I* understand the concept, and refer to that Power as God—weaves people into and out of our lives. Second, it was another exercise in my asking for what I wanted, in preserving a bond with my dying friend.

Ask for what you want. When I was a boy I rarely got any toys. Now I'm well over fifty and we have this thing in our society. When we're older we hold birthday parties where people bring you black balloons and stuff and half-kid about getting older and all. I don't want that, and I tell my friends. I tell them on birthdays and at Christmas. At Christmas I write a letter to Santa—and give it to my wife. Then she tells my friends what I want. And what do I want? Toys. My stuffed animals. Baseball stuff. It's neat—to me. And I'm the only one I have to please.

And *DO* what you want. A couple was getting married and came to me, asked me to give an opinion. They had both given up alcohol. She didn't want any at the wedding, but he did. Well, he did sort of. Personally he didn't. But he thought that having an open bar was expected. I asked, *Expected by whom?* He said, of course, *The guests.* I told him to do what *he* wanted. Not what the guests *expected.* It was the couple's wedding, not a spectacle, not their families' wedding, not their friends' wedding, but theirs. It should be an expression of them. Period.

Back in 1977 I ran a half-way house for substance abusers in South Philadelphia. The first resident was slightly mentally impaired. Back then he was also an alcoholic. He actually drove his car up on the doorstep—he was drunk—and we had to coax it back down so we could admit him through the door. He went to a twenty-eight day resident program to detox. In fact, it was near a river, and when he heard that he took his fishing rod. It made sense to him. And so did some of things they told him there. Like getting his own needs met.

He's been sober almost twenty years now and very proud of it. In fact he wants to celebrate every anniversary of sobriety. He came to our place on October 17, 1977. So now every year on October 17 he orders a cake—it says Happy Anniversary on it— picks it up, and drives to our place at noon sharp. He has no idea who's going to be there. He doesn't care. He knows whoever is will celebrate with him. And so he does, cuts the cake and all.

Hey, they had told him that if he wants a healthy celebration, go for it. So he does. He doesn't expect anybody else to make a big deal out of his day. He does it for himself. Simple minded? Well, he found a simple solution to getting his need met. Compare him to the so many of us who get all bent out of shape because other people don't remember our special days, like our birthdays. You want them to remember? Remind them. Want to make sure you get a party? Throw one.

THE OTHER BUMPER STICKER

Let me sum this up. Parent yourself. Get your own needs met. Ask. Do. Do NOT wait for a knight in shining armor to come along. Usually when they do the armor is tarnished, or it's so heavy they wind up falling off their horse or something. I think you know what I mean.

Get off the crazy codependent game. Stop looking for external relationships to make you complete and happy. You hear it in songs: *You are my life! You are my all! You are my everything!* THAT IS SICK!

The only relationship you should worry about is the one with yourself. All the others flow from that. *You* are your life. *You* are your everything and all. If you believe in a Higher Power, it's just you and that power. Everything else flows from that. Take care of yourself and everything else will fall into place.

We're going to move in the next chapter to Affirmation principles. We're going to go back to the Fake It Till You Make It idea. As a prelude, here are two more assignments.

First, for the next seven nights, before you go to bed, look into a mirror, into your own eyes, and tell yourself you are special, you are beautiful, and you love yourself just the way you are. Then kiss yourself in the mirror. Don't faint, now. If you try it, it's called an affirmation. It's quite an experience. And you don't have to let anybody else know what you're doing. Just close the door and have privacy. You're allowed.

Second, write a love letter to yourself. Then mail it. Think of it. In three days or so you'll get a love letter in the mail. Some of us have wanted one all our lives. Now they can get one. There's a point to that, too, something many people experience when they do it. We'll talk about that. But forget looking for big, psychological reasons. Just do it to have fun, to *affirm* yourself.

You see, there's that old, depressing bumper sticker: LIFE'S A BITCH THEN YOU DIE.

And there's that other bumper sticker: IT'S NEVER TOO LATE TO HAVE A HAPPY CHILDHOOD.

Affirmations

STRENGTHENING YOUR ADULT

For those of you who did the exercise with the mirror, many, if not most, probably found it uncomfortable. Why? Why is it uncomfortable to give ourselves a little affirmation? Basically because we're not used to it. Remember when we talked about our "defaults," our stress behaviors, we used the analogy of the computer. We have been programmed, and bought into the programming, of accepting the negative about ourselves, and about life in general. To take the analogy further, it's as though we have what I call "tapes" that run our programs. I call them the *old* tapes. The cynical tapes. The critical tapes. The negative tapes. When you do affirmations, what you're doing is challenging the message on those tapes. And they won't simply go away. They resist the challenge, the reprogramming. The old message is in conflict with the new. And it's that conflict that makes you feel uncomfortable.

That's why when people ask about doing their Inner Child work, about tackling their issues, I advise that they work on themselves *as they are* first. Strengthen your adult self. Make the Adult strong before you work on the Child. Think of it. A simple affirmation makes you uncomfortable, causes conflict. What do you think tackling major issues will do to you? It will most likely cause you to relapse into your defaults, your stress behaviors, your addictions, and all the depression and anxiety and other insanity that go with them. You will identify your issues, but you will not be coming from a healthy perspective, and you will not have the strength to deal with them. You'll wind up blaming people, carrying resentment and anger and rage and all sorts of other powerful negative feelings into your present life, when the only purpose to identifying your issues is to learn from them, heal them, and make your life more peaceful and happy.

If you still doubt the strength of the old tapes, consider a few other things. Some of you couldn't even try the simple affirmation exercise. We use the excuse *It's silly* or *It's too basic, I can skip it*. Then what's the harm in trying a simple silly or basic exercise? It would only take a minute. What do you have to lose? The real reason for the resistance is that it is *threatening*. Giving a simple affirmation to ourselves is threatening.

The old tapes program us toward the negative. For example, if you go through a typical day, a pretty nice day, with no particular problems, then have a problem, say, from 7 to 8 that night, I guarantee what you'll talk about the next day. You will focus on that hour. You will forget the other twenty-three. Or take another example. What attracts crowds, the healthy, positive things in our lives? No. It's usually the bizarre, the crazy, the murder, tragedies, and mayhem that attract us. Just look at a news broadcast. We broadcast tragedies. We do it in the mass media. And we do it in our personal lives. In my own experience I try to resist being drawn to the negative. And it takes effort.

As a last example, I go back to my grammar school experience. Back in the 40's, if you misbehaved, the teacher was likely to have you go to the blackboard and write a hundred times—or *five hundred* times—"I am a bad boy." I'll tell you a secret. If you write something like that long enough you will be convinced that you are, in fact, bad. If they really wanted to help me, they should have told me to write that I was a beautiful, wonderful person. At the end of it I probably would not have gotten into so much trouble anymore.

There was an experiment in education where they took a class and changed its entire profile. As it was graduating from one grade to the next, they told the new teacher that the better students were the slower learners and vice versa, that the well-behaved children were the problems and vice versa. And guess what? The kids began to act as the teacher expected. In terms of our analogy, what they basically did there was to create "tapes" of the children, then everybody listened to the tapes and acted accordingly, until it finally affected the children themselves.

So what we need to do as part of strengthening our adult selves is to challenge the old tapes. But I have another secret to share with you. The old tapes, the old messages we carry inside about ourselves, will not go away. They have been part of our history and the core of our lives for a long time. What we need to do is create new tapes about ourselves and play them louder and longer than the old ones. It's an old concept. It's called brainwashing. You play the new tapes long enough and loud enough and they and their positive message will take over.

And here's something really neat to consider. Most of you know already that no matter what your history is you have done the best you can, you are a good person, you can change and grow. That belief will respond very quickly to your affirmations. Of course, there will be things, old messages, that won't be so easy to overcome. That's OK, too, part of the *process* of Recovery. Remind yourself again please: *Recovery is a PROCESS. For* those stubborn messages, you can use another approach, the old *Fake it till you make it!*

But before we get into some affirmation techniques, let's look at three principles that make affirmations effective.

THREE BASIC PRINCIPLES

These are very simple. First, an affirmation is a *totally* positive statement. For example, a major issue in my own life is guilt. I do not approach it by saying *I am not guilty*. That still carries the negative concept of guilt. I should approach it on a positive level with something like *I am an innocent, gentle, beautiful person*. What an affirmation does is accentuate the positive.

Second: Repetition. Don't look for magic. If you start right now saying affirmations, will your whole attitude change overnight? It doesn't work that way. And I'll let you in on a secret. It might get worse before it gets better. There is one counselor who advises that getting into issues and affirmations is like trying to clean out a garbage pile. Left alone, the pile stinks. But it stinks even more when you stir it up and start to get to the bottom. The stink, the negative feelings, come from the conflict of your old messages with the new. But repetition will overcome that. To finish the analogy of the garbage pile, keep cleaning and soon the odor is gone. Stick with your affirmations. The same counselor used to give a formula for effective change. He would advise you to do the positive things *Regularly, Over A Long Period of Time, and With Respect*.

Third, one of the most powerful ways of doing affirmations is through the subconscious. We'll explore this more when we cover techniques of affirmations, but basically why we work through the subconscious is because there our defenses, our walls, are down. We are open and vulnerable in the subconscious, particularly when we are asleep. Because when we are sleeping we are totally open to hearing and receiving messages.

Now let's look at a few proven techniques for affirmations, and I'll give you examples of how different people have used them effectively.

AFFIRMATION TECHNIQUES

Self Statements

The first technique I want to share is the one I already suggested: Tell yourself you are a good, beautiful person. Say it before you go to bed and when you wake up every morning. If you want to have some fun with it, look at yourself in the mirror when you say it and give your mirror image a kiss. What's it going to take, a minute or two? If it makes you uncomfortable at first, if you have a hard time believing the message, fake it. Fake it till you make it. Because soon you will start to believe it.

Let me inject a word here. No matter what comes up to challenge this message that you are, in fact, a good, beautiful person—whether that challenge comes from things you've done or things you were told about yourself—you know your own circumstances. You know that you've tried your best, and you know that you were created exactly as you were supposed to be. You are looking for *Progress* not *Perfection.*

And to show you how effective this affirmation technique can be, I use the example of two school teachers. One is a woman I know, a first grade teacher. She tried an experiment and shared it with me. Every morning she would have her students go to a mirror and say, "You're special, you're beautiful, and I love you." At first, the kids would do things like run to the mirror and say it fast and run back to their seats, or they would cover their eyes when they said it. They were very uncomfortable. But she had them stick with it. And she said that after about six months there was a profound change. Now they would almost fight to get to the mirror, and some of them really hammed it up. It was actually hard to get them away from the mirror. They went from shyness about it to feeling good about themselves because of this simple affirmation.

And there was another teacher I knew. My own second grade teacher, Sister Philippia, God rest her soul. In contrast to most of the other teachers in that time and place, she believed in affirming the positive with children. She focused on the positive, even when we made mistakes. Her constant message to us was that we were good and lovable and beautiful. She was an amazing lady. She believed that kids were impressionistic and so would particularly respond to affirmations. Her whole philosophy of life revolved around affirmation. And when I reflect back today, she is one of the people I credit for much of the positive in my life, particularly my getting into recovery. It's amazing how messengers are sent into our lives at different times, and how the seeds they plant grow and bloom at different stages in our lives.

Love Letters to Self

Another technique we already touched on is writing yourself a love letter. And mail it to yourself. You can even pick a day each month to write a letter, then at the end of the year, guess what?, you have twelve letters. Like the other techniques, it's usually awkward and uncomfortable at first. Some people told me that when they started they had a hard time writing only a line or two—and at that they were faking it. But as time went by, they got used it. The letters got longer and more detailed, and they started seeing things about themselves that they had overlooked before. In my own case, my wife added something to my exercise. She told me to save the letters in a shoe box. Sometimes when I'm having a bad day now, I go into the box and read some of the letters. When you're down on yourself, they can actually lift your spirits. But repetition is the key. Try it and stick with it.

Affirming Letters from Others

A variation on the love letter is to pick some people close to you and ask them to send you an affirming letter. I use this in my group work, after people get comfortable with one another. It does work. If you don't believe your own affirmations of yourself, you will believe other people when they start listing the good things they see in you. I tell the groups to ask for the positive only, not the negative. If that seems too much like fantasy, let me share this with you.

A friend of mine had a foster daughter. From the turmoil in her young life—she was only about six—she was down on herself, blaming herself for things over which she had absolutely no control, like the breakup of her parents. With a little encouragement she started affirming herself, and that spread till she would look in the mirror and say how pretty she was. My friend was concerned that she might be getting too positive, might start overlooking her faults. He consulted a counselor and got some good advice. The counselor said not to worry about it, the child would get enough negative messages in life, the positive beliefs she was developing would only strengthen her.

I can also tell you from my groups that people have shared some moving experiences from the letter techniques. For example, some have said that when they started writing to themselves it was as though they were seeing themselves from a whole other perspective, finally seeing that there was much more to themselves than just the things they had come to accept as their identities. And many, many were surprised when others wrote them letters and they saw all the positive things that others saw in them, things that they really didn't give themselves credit for.

Like the love letters I keep, these letters from others can also help you tremendously when you're having a bad day. I experience this myself, thanks again to my wife. As a lecturer and counselor, I often get cards and letters and notes thanking me for things and pointing out things I did that were helpful to different people. I used to read them and discard them, until my wife pointed out that I had an affirmation gold mine in them. So I put them into the box with my love letters and read them every so often, especially when I'm down.

Indications from Your Physical Ailments

This is an interesting technique. It's based on the theory that your physical ailments have roots in your emotions. To do this I use a book by Louise Hay, *Heal Your Body,* in which she lists ailments, their emotional causes, and affirmations you can use to overcome them. Her approach basically acknowledges that Body,

Mind, and Spirit are all connected. It's really not important if you believe in the philosophy or not. The exercise is a structured way to learn how to write affirmations.

Make a list of the physical ailments you have experienced in your life. They could be anything: chronic headaches; stroke; arthritis...Look them up in the book and write down the affirmations prescribed for each one. At the end of the exercise you'll probably have a long list of ailments and affirmations. Now notice something. When you review the affirmations, the same ones will pop up more than others. Those are the ones you should work with. For example, if you look up addictions, like obesity and overeating, or drug addiction and alcoholism, you'll find a common root. The affirmations center around loving yourself and accepting yourself. Addictions are rooted in low self esteem, a negative way of looking at yourself.

Your Personal Tape

Now, with all the affirmations you gather, there is another technique: make your personal tape. This is your own voice on tape giving yourself affirmations. Start with your own name and a simple message, as, in my case, "Vince, I love you. Vince, you are special. Vince, you are beautiful." Repeat it a few times to start the tape off. Then read your love letters into the tape. Then read all the other affirmations you have gathered—from yourself and other people—into the tape. Play the tape to yourself for at least thirty consecutive days. Why thirty? Because you need to give it enough time to work.

Now, if you want to get creative, play the tape at least twice a day, when you get up and before you go to bed. Or get an auto-reverse tape and play it to yourself when you're sleeping. Remember, when you're sleeping, your defenses are down, your subconscious is open to suggestion. It doesn't have to be loud. Play the tape quietly. The message will sink in.

Some people get very creative with this. They add music to the tape. And some who play an instrument actually sing their affirmations into the tape. Some use poetry. Others use creativity in their prose. I know one man who uses various techniques. As of last count, he told me he has thirty-two affirmation tapes in his own voice! However you do it, make it comfortable for yourself. As we said, at first, you might wake up feeling a little worse than when you started, because the old messages are clashing with the new. But after a while the new messages will take over. We've actually done studies on this, and it seems that the process is a lot like detoxing from a physical substance. After the first seventy-two hours or so, the process begins to work. It might take longer. It might be a slow process. But it does begin to work.

Create Affirmation Times

We already referred to this when we talked about doing affirmations morning and evening. But don't stop there. During the day you can take affirmation breaks. Stop what you're doing and give yourself some affirmations. This is similar to the precepts of certain religions, like periodic prayer or little meditative breaks. In my own case, I'm a morning person. I get up early every day and love the time I have to myself from about 5:30 to 6:30 or so. It's quiet time, my time, and I use some of it to do my affirmations. During the day, I take short breaks, sometimes less than a minute, just enough time to stop for an affirmation. I also take longer breaks, as I'll mention in the next section.

I can also use the example of a woman I know. When her kids misbehave, she has them take short affirmation breaks, has them write down some affirmations about themselves. She gets some good results. And, as she says, it's better than her screaming and yelling at them and reacting in all kinds of other negative ways, while it helps the children settle down in a positive way.

In short, repetition is important. And timing is important. It's really common sense. So often we push ourselves, drive ourselves, or let other people or circumstances drive us. It's like a basketball team. The other team makes a run at them, what do they do? Take a time out. Refocus. Before they're overwhelmed.

Compare that to being in a traffic jam. What do so many of us do? Fume over something we can't control. We're stuck physically. But we're hardly stuck mentally. Use the time for something positive, for some affirmations. They're better than anxiety attacks. And, again, don't forget that time before bed. You want to get ready for restful sleep, not for turmoil. For example, if you're going to watch Freddy Kruger or some other ghoul, guess what? You might wind up dreaming about him. After all, that's the last relationship you had before you went to bed. The things you program into the last hour of your day are probably the things you will end up processing in your subconscious while you are sleeping. In my own case, aside from my tapes and other affirmations, I also use a little book of meditations, called *Night Light*, to relax myself and set my mind straight before I go to bed. I am not endorsing any particular book or other product. There are many such books you can use.

Create Affirmation Environments

Create places to do your affirmations. A lot of this one I learned from children. Ever see how children fight to get their own room, their own space? Then they decorate it with posters and pictures and all kinds of stuff, and I'll tell you an open secret in psychology. When you go into a room and look at a person's stuff, it tells you a lot about that person. I've had people come to me after they found out their kids were into drugs and say how surprised they were that they didn't see it before. After all, the kids had the drug paraphernalia and all sorts of other crazy stuff in their rooms. It's like the room itself was shouting to them. And this works both ways. You can create a positive, affirming environment, and it doesn't have to be fancy.

Let me give you some examples. At home, our children grew up and moved out, and we had some extra room. So I created my own space in one. I put all my baseball stuff in it, my stuffed animals, and everything else I like. I called it my Little Kid's Room. It spoke of me, of what I like. And I hang a sign on the door: My Room, Keep Out. When I need a break, it's the perfect place. And at work I have a place. I'm the director of a counseling center with over forty counselors. It gets nuts. And I can't hide in my office because people come, politely or not, barging in. So I just find little places to disappear to. Sometimes I excuse myself and go into the bathroom. In our old office, I would go into our walk-in book closet. My secretary would cover for me when I was in there. She would tell people I was busy and would be out in a few minutes. And I would be available after a few minutes. But in that time I could do an affirmation, say a prayer, read something, just settle down.

Also, once you create your affirmation space, your personal space, don't give it up just because you get into a relationship. If you want, you can create a space that is conducive to both of you. And, naturally, you can only do this if you create it together.

Subliminal Tapes

You can buy these off the shelf. They're a good way to start if you feel funny about making your own tapes, or you can use them in conjunction with your own. They call them subliminal because they give messages that you can't consciously hear. The messages are dubbed at different speeds from the background music. It's an idea taken from advertising, used for years to sell products to consumers. In fact, in many places it is illegal now, since it seems to give an edge to the advertisers. They give consumers messages without them knowing it—and the products being pushed seem to sell. So it does seem to be effective. For example, in the supermarket, under the music constantly playing, there are often subliminal messages to buy certain things. You don't consciously hear them; they are dubbed at speeds that make them unintelligible to your conscious hearing. But they sink into the subconscious.

I have two rules for subliminal tapes. First, make sure they are legitimate. There are many bootlegged tapes around. The problem with them, aside from their being illegal, is that you cannot bootleg a subliminal tape without the proper equipment, since they involve different speeds for the background music and the subliminal message. Second, choose one with the right message for you. How? Read the jacket. A legitimate tape will have a proper cover describing the contents.

There are tapes that play music over the subliminal messages. There are others with relaxing sounds, like ocean waves, a gentle rain, things to that effect. With your physical ear you hear those sounds. With your subconscious you hear the subliminal message. They are excellent for when you are relaxing or sleeping. But here's a warning. Do not use them when driving or operating machinery or engaging in other activities that require your attention, because they have a tendency to mellow you out and take your attention elsewhere.

I have two in particular that I like to use, both personally and in my groups. And people in my groups seem to use them to good effect. One is *Nurturing Your Inner Child. The* other is *Waking Up In the Morning.* As I noted before, I am not endorsing these particular tapes or any other products. I am just using them as an example. Any good music store or even the national book stores now have a wide selection of subliminal tapes.

IN SUMMARY: *BE CREATIVE!*

Be as creative as you want with your affirmations. Have fun with them. Some people I know make affirmation crib cards that they carry with them and check during the day. Some people play their personal affirmation tapes while driving—not the subliminal tapes, but the ones they made with their own voices. Some use affirmations in their relationships, particularly parenting. Think of that. They make a tape in their own voice for their children, with all sorts of affirmations about the children, and they play it at night while the children are sleeping. The children spend the whole night listening to the parents' voices telling them how good and innocent and beautiful they are. It doesn't even make any difference that they play it very quietly. The message sinks in. And the parents don't make a big deal about it. Many don't even tell their children they are doing it. They just do it and let the results show for themselves.

You can also make affirmations part of the events in your life. My wife and I played subliminal tapes in the background during our wedding. They helped accentuate the nice, positive tone of the entire ceremony. In some cultures, affirmations are used in the connection of body, mind, and spirit in relationships. For example, in certain Chinese philosophies, people in relationships have exercises they do with each other in which they physically and even sexually say good morning and good night to each other, and join in different forms of prayer.

When you're working on affirmations, you are investing in yourself. You are programming positive stuff inside of you. You will look at life more positively. Environment, tapes, time for self...They are all simple things, just as a hammer or saw or chisel is a simple tool. Affirmations are the simple tools you use to replace the old, negative messages about yourself with the new and the positive.

A FAMILY OF ORIGIN EXERCISE

OK. For those of you who are dying to get to your "issues" and Inner Child, we have come to the Fifth Stage of Recovery. So knock your sox off! But I'm going to caution you again: Make sure you work on the first four before you tackle five. And just *reading* about the first four isn't *working* on them. Recovery isn't a head trip. It's a process, remember? Something that has to sink into your gut.

So, *AFTER* you

1. Develop self-awareness
2. Build a healthy support system
3. Learn how to parent yourself; and
4. Learn how to affirm yourself,

you can start looking at your Family of Origin through a simple exercise.

Sit down with a paper and pencil, say a prayer to your Higher Power, if you believe in one, and write your personal history from as far back as you can remember to age twelve. No matter what comes to you, write it down. Positive, negative, no matter what. Write it down. Don't ask anyone to help you. Don't ask brothers or sisters or friends or other family members what they remember. You are dealing with your perceptions, not theirs. You see, if there were eight children in your family, or ten, and I asked each of you to write your perceptions of the family, I will get eight or ten different versions of events. Everyone has their own perceptions, their own experience. What is important is that you see what your own perceptions are.

Also, don't beat yourself up if you don't remember much, if there are a lot of blanks. People tell me all the time that they have blanks in their lives, periods for which they don't remember much. It's OK. It just means that you are not supposed to remember at this time. The things you do remember are the things you are ready to work on. Zip. Period. That's all. And we'll start working on them in the next chapter.

Family of Origin

APPROACHING THE PROCESS

*A*FTER you work on the first four Stages of Recovery, you are ready to *BEGIN* looking at your inner issues, which we call Family of Origin work. This is the Fifth Stage of Recovery. Note the emphasis on the two words, "after" and "begin." I compared the process of recovering from codependency to surgery. If you have surgery, you must be strong enough for it, or you will not survive the operation. So you "prep" for it. You make yourself strong enough to survive the operation. Recovery is very similar. The first four stages prep you for the fifth and sixth, the actual surgery and healing. Also, I say BEGIN to work on Family of Origin issues because the work is not an event. It is a process. It is ongoing.

Further, before you approach the work, you must have the right attitude, a positive attitude. You are doing Family of Origin work to learn from your past and move on in your growth process. If you approach it with a negative attitude, you will only hurt yourself more than you have ever been hurt. You will fall into the Blame Game, the Victim Game, blaming others for how you are now. You will become obsessed with the people whom you perceive as having hurt you. You will become obsessed with your issues. You will, in many ways, *become* your issues. I mentioned before that you sometimes meet people who are like this. You say Hello, and they start telling you about their issues. They have no life, no focus, other than their issues. So, as you begin your Family of Origin work, keep the basic principle in mind that the only reason you are doing the work is to *learn* from it.

It helps to keep in mind that even the most dysfunctional situations in your life can become your teachers. For example, in my own life, I suffered what we call a nervous breakdown and had to be hospitalized. As painful as the experience was, I now realize that it actually planted the seeds of my recovery. It is part of my personal history. I learned from it and use it to grow even today.

Further, let's go back yet again to the word "process." Family of Origin work takes time. Don't think that what you read in the next few pages is something you can do by midnight tonight! I see too much of that. We get into recovery and we get very intense, very impatient. We want everything to happen and fall into place *FAST,* especially if it was depression or anxiety or other intense pain that led us to this process. But, again, recovery is not an event, not a "magic bullet" cure that happens overnight. Remember the fundamental principle that we joke about. It says that basically we learn all of our patterns and foundations in the first ten years of our lives. Then we spend the next eighty years working on them. We joke about it—but it's no joke. That's about how it works. *That does not mean* that you stay sick and unhappy and depressed and anxious as you go through a lengthy process. Basically, the process will bring you peace of mind and free you from the negative, and you continue with it to lift you from there.

Finally, I use a Twelve Step model in my Family of Origin work, so from time to time I'll be referring very briefly to some of the Steps.

YOUR PERCEPTIONS, YOUR ISSUES

When you do your Family of Origin work, you are basically looking back at your childhood, and then beyond, for two reasons. First, to identify your patterns, foundations, and issues. Second, to *give yourself permission to heal. The* second point, as we already touched on, is important. Many of us, if not all of us, need feedback about our thoughts and feelings. We need to have them validated. Then we can move on from there to the process of healing. Since no one has given us that feedback, that *permission*, we must give it to ourselves.

And when you look back at your patterns, foundations, and issues, you are dealing with what you remember about your childhood—with your *perceptions. Your* perceptions. And there are some basic things to keep in mind as you go through the process.

First, as I mentioned in the last chapter, don't ask anyone else about *their* perceptions of your family. If I take eight siblings and ask them for their perceptions of their family, I will get eight different stories. Every child perceives the family differently. Let me share an example. A man I know viewed his mother as being controlling, smothering, possessive, and manipulative. His perception was that she did not give him his own space and distance when he was growing up. His cousin, on the other hand, viewed the same mother quite differently. The cousin came from an alcoholic home. Her father was a violent alcoholic, her mother an extremely angry person. The cousin did not experience any attention, warmth, or affection at home. So whenever she came to the man's house, she loved it, because the man's mother, in her smothering way, gave her all the attention she craved. To the cousin, the man's mother was the epitome of nurturing. That was her perception. And when she hears the man complain about his mother, even today, she basically tells him he's crazy, his mother was the salt of the earth. Different perceptions.

Second, it is common for people approaching family work to start doubting themselves, doubting their memories. They follow this by thinking that if they can't be sure their memories are accurate, their work won't be valid. Forget that. It doesn't make any difference if your perceptions are accurate or real. They are real for you. They are what has been driving you into and keeping you in your codependency. So it is them that you have to deal with.

Third, people complain that they don't remember very much, and they think that this will lessen the effect of their work. Forget that, too. You remember what you are supposed to remember, when you are supposed to remember it. Zip. Period. End of discussion. Your mind will only show you what you are ready to handle.

And in regard to the last point, let's go over something again. In doing your family work, you will be resurrecting *FEELINGS. In* many cases, unpleasant feelings, like depression, anxiety, sadness, anger...But remember that this time they are not being resurrected so they can hang onto you indefinitely and sour your life. This time, you are bringing them up to process them and throw them out, so you can heal.

The beginning of the process is called an Inventory. It is your personal history. I have found the following method, or technique, to be extremely effective.

AN INVENTORY TECHNIQUE

As I asked you to do at the end of the last chapter, you should write your inventory. Start by finding a quiet place. Block out the time. And remind yourself that the only reason you are doing this work is to learn from it and grow and move on. It is a spiritual exercise. Spiritual does not mean religious. Spiritual means related to growth, the growth of your own, personal spirit.

If you believe in a higher power, say a prayer to that power to guide you. If you don't believe in one, tell your own mind to open your heart and your memory. Then write down everything you remember from your first consciousness in life up to the age of ten or twelve. A good cut-off for this first segment is the end of grammar school. But there are no hard and fast rules regarding this.

It doesn't make any difference if it comes out in order, chronologically.

Your grammar and penmanship don't have to be perfect. This is much more than some kind of test.

Ignore any blocks or blanks. What you don't remember, don't worry about.

If it feels uncomfortable, ignore that, too, and work through the feelings.

Don't censor what you write. Write what you remember.

Good codependents like us tend to drive ourselves crazy with worries like the ones I just mentioned. They are not important in this exercise. Which is not to say that the exercise is not important, that it will not resurrect strong feelings.

That's the first part of the technique. *Write* your history down. Don't try to *think* it, because then you will try to analyze it. If you do this properly, you will be doing what the Twelve Step Program refers to as a "fearless moral inventory."

And remember, when you write your perceptions down, you are actually bringing them up *and* getting them out of yourself.

SHARE YOUR INVENTORY WITH SAFE PEOPLE

This is why Stage Two of the recovery process is so important. If you really did that stage, you have some people you feel safe with, that you can now share your inventory with. Sharing means you will read it to them. In good group work, you will also hear *their* stories. This is a technique that I use with my client groups. We might start out with fifteen in a group. After some weeks, we have maybe six or seven—whom I call the die-hards, the ones who stuck with it; the others simply weren't ready for the process. The "die-hard" group feels comfortable enough together to share their inventories. They take turns reading them. This is important for two reasons.

First, the act of reading is an act of opening up, of releasing feelings, which is a key to the healing process.

Second, reading to a group and then listening to their stories demonstrates to you that your problems and issues are not so unique. Sharing with a safe group gives you perspective. But, more important, sharing with your group is like sharing with your family, your Recovery Family, which is a healthy family. You will be allowed to express your feelings without criticism. You will experience unconditional acceptance and love. Your perceptions will be validated. In short, you will get from your Recovery Family the things you sought but never received from your Family of Origin. And this is a crucial part of the healing process as well. Basically, did you ever walk away from a family issue asking, "Is it me? Am I crazy? Doesn't anybody else here see the dysfunctionality I am experiencing?" With your Recovery Family, you will be working with other people who will give you the answers: It is not you, you are not crazy for feeling what you are feeling, and they see the dysfunctionality you have seen in your own experience.

In Twelve Step work, you would share your inventory with your sponsor, who is someone you choose, with their agreement. If you are not in a Twelve Step program and do not feel comfortable sharing the negative part of your inventory with even your Recovery Family, you should find a good therapist, but one who is trained in this type of technique. The reason is that you must feel comfortable with the process, otherwise it will only add to your negative feelings. I cannot emphasize this enough. You only do what is comfortable for you.

PHOTOGRAPHS HELP THE PROCESS

If you can, as you do your inventory, dig up some photographs of that time in your life. Photos are often an uncensored record of you and your family. They tell a lot about you and your experience. For example, in my own case, I notice something about my childhood photos. I was always perfect in them, nothing out of place. It helped me later in therapy in realizing that one of my issues was striving for perfection. I had tried to be the perfect child, the perfect son, and later the perfect adult, the perfect clergyman, whatever. Everything in my old photos is posed. There are none in which I am just playing, just relaxing, just having fun.

COMPOSING LISTS FOR JOURNALING

After writing and sharing your inventory, I want you to compose three lists from it. The first is a list of all the negative persons, places, and things in that part of your life. The second is a list of the issues you experienced during that period. For example, some of them might be fear, abuse, abandonment, guilt, and shame. By the way, guilt and shame, as we'll get into, are two entirely different things. The third list covers the positive persons, places, and things during that period of your life.

Just coming this far in the process, you might begin to experience something different. You might have been looking at your childhood as all negative, but you'll realize that there were positive influences as well. You will be gaining a sense of balance, which is part of the recovery process. You will even have positive feelings about the negative people, places, and things in your life. In fact, some of these may appear on both your positive and negative list. For example, one person related that he had several negative perceptions and issues regarding his father. He had basically felt abandoned by his father. But in composing the lists, he also realized several positive things that he hadn't considered before. His father had worked hard for the family, and in his own way had expressed his love for his son.

In my own case, in the mix of some deep negative feelings about my childhood, I also started to see some very positive things. In the issue of my schooling, for example, while many of the nuns and teachers generated negative impressions, like fear and anxiety, there was the one, whom I have already mentioned, my second grade nun, who was always so positive, always expressing love, always focusing on that. The memory of her resurrected such good feelings in me that I now think of her as something of a guardian angel in my recovery, and I even visited her grave in Baltimore just to say a prayer and thank her.

But to proceed with the process, once you have your lists, you can start journaling, which is, basically, letter writing. I do this by opening two separate notebooks. I call them simply my positive book and negative book. Start by going to your negative list and writing a letter in the negative book to each person, place, and thing on that list.

DO NOT MAIL THESE LETTERS!!!

Let me repeat: Do not mail these letters. Don't give them to people. They are not about other people. They are about *you!* What you are doing by writing is giving the child within you permission to express your feelings, to release your feelings and eventually let them go.

I hear the question many, many times: Why can't I give these letters to the people involved? We have a very simple philosophy concerning this. The only time you do this exercise directly with other individuals is when you and they are in recovery—and if they are willing to openly participate in the process with you. That way, it will be a healthy experience for both of you. All other forms of confrontation are done under the guidance of a therapist.

There are other principles involved in this exercise as well. Write your negative letters first. And always follow your negative letters with positive ones. For example, if you write a negative letter to your mother, you put it into your negative journal, thereby releasing it from inside of you. You then immediately go to your positive journal and write another letter to your mother.

But what if you can't feel anything positive just then? Fake it. Till you make it. Just write something like, "Dear mom, I love you." And sign it. Why? Two reasons. First, you always want to end on a positive note, leave the positive for yourself. Second, the purpose of the exercise is to heal.

Sometimes we have experienced terrible things at the hands of other people: incest, rape, emotional abuse...How can we write something positive to them? A positive letter in those cases might say something like, "What you did was terrible, but it taught me to be strong." It's like the old biblical passage about loving our enemies. I used to have a very hard time with that until I explored it further. It doesn't say that you have to *like* your enemies—or what they did. It doesn't say that you have to associate with them. It just says love them. And the Big Book of AA takes it a little further: Love Them; Pray for Them; Let Them Go. The hardest thing for us to do is to let go of people, places, and things. This exercise will help you let go of the negative...And hold onto the positive.

You can even use this method in everyday situations. Say you have a fight with your spouse. You can journal the negative and the positive. Let go of the negative. Keep the positive. What you are experiencing is the fact that because of a fight or disagreement you do not throw out the positive with the negative. You have undoubtedly seen this yourself. A couple gets into an argument and they caught up in it. They *react*. It turns into a shouting match, and they start bringing up everything negative that happened over the past twenty years. Then they're beating each other to death with the negative. Yes, they have issues. We all have issues. But the trick is to remember the positive and *keep* the positive while getting rid of the negative.

And remember...I asked that you keep separate journals: positive and negative. I'm going to show you something else to do to emphasize getting rid of the one and keeping the other.

And to go back for a second, I'd like to repeat that clearing out the negative might lead to some deep positive feelings you didn't even know existed. People in therapy often experience this as they work on their issues, get rid of old, negative, mental and emotional baggage. Life in general starts looking brighter, and they actually report feeling positive, nostalgic feelings that they never experienced before about past events. It's like, brush away the dirt and see the diamond shine.

You also apply the negative/positive journaling technique to your list of issues. For example, look at addiction. You can write in your negative journal all the unhealthy things that addiction did to you. But, in your positive journal, you can also write the healthy things that the addiction led you to, like recovery and discovering my inner strengths, like learning to set boundaries and limits. In the process, you are allowing your negative issues to become your teacher, and you are identifying the positive things you got from these issues. You are training to look at life through the eyes of learning so that you can heal and make peace. If you don't, then what you do is carry the negative around with you. For example, say your mother is deceased and you still have negative issues that affect you involving her. What you are actually doing is giving a dead person control of your present life, just as though she is still alive inside of you.

As for your positive list, it's obvious what to do with it. Write a positive letter in your journal to each person, place, and thing on the list. That's for you to keep as well. I knew a woman once who wrote a positive letter of gratitude to a pet she had when she was a child. It was a beautiful letter to her pet dog. It was amazing. It was almost as though her Higher Power had sent that pet into her life at just that time to keep her sane and help her deal with some very trying situations. I do believe that's how it works. I believe we have certain spiritual messengers sent into our lives when they are supposed to be there to help us cope and learn.

Before moving on in the process to an interesting "therapy," I'd like to repeat the answer to a question I hear a lot: Yes, you can have some of the same people, places, and things on both your positive and negative lists. You still write them one of each type of letter. And the following "therapy" will show you what to do next.

CEMETERY THERAPY

Cemeteries are very therapeutic places, which is why we recommend the next step in the journaling process: Cemetery Therapy. Cemeteries are ending places, places where you say good-bye. They are very clear, very concrete. They are also a very good place to get rid of your negative letters, as follows.

First, take all of your negative letters and refer back to your second stage of recovery. Go to your Recovery Family and have someone, or various people, act as surrogates. Read them the letters. Release them and let them go.

Next, take the letters and bury them or burn them. This is the "cemetery" aspect. One woman I know actually has what she calls her recovery graveyard in her back yard. When she's done with a negative letter, she takes it there and buries it. Once in a while, she even puts a flower there—just like visiting a grave, to remind herself that the negative that is buried is gone. Other people burn the letters. The point is to go through a concrete act of letting go.

Now, a word to good codependents who own a computer. Don't back up the negative letters on your hard drive so you can go back to them "just in case." There is no "just in case." There is just letting go.

Is it the end of the process? Will all your issues suddenly die? No. In fact, you might repeat your inventory later. It depends on you. But, if you do repeat it, each time you will have a different insight and let more of the negative go.

Finally, I want to reference the Ninth Step of the Twelve Step Program. It says that in everything you do in life make sure that you don't injure yourself or anyone else. As applied specifically to journaling, this means that the process is not about beating yourself or others up. Which is why we say do not mail your negative letters, do not throw them up in anybody's face. There was a woman in one of my groups once who didn't listen to this advice. She made a package of her negative letters and took them with her to her family's Thanksgiving dinner. She placed a letter at each plate to get her feelings about her family out in the open. Talk about being sick! Then she wondered why the family wanted her to leave.

The purpose of journaling is to heal. Recovery is not about punishing. It is about letting go. It's interesting how in my own case I saw how we carry around so much emotional baggage, sometimes without even knowing it. And, when we finally do know it, it's hard to let go. I remember back in 1984 going to a therapist because of my eating disorder. I can still hear him, clear as a bell, telling me, "Vince, you're carrying so much anger and resentment inside of you, and your eating disorder won't go away until you deal with it, release it." I also remember literally telling the man he was nuts because I had never been angry at anything in my entire life.

I was in fact one of the angriest, most resentful people on the face of the earth. I was carrying so much inside of me. I was manifesting it through my eating disorder, literally embalming myself with food so I wouldn't feel it. And I didn't have a clue.

Even today, as the Step Program says, I try to stay on top of my anger and other feelings every day. It's a good practice, as we've already said. You have a fight with your spouse, your significant other, or your kids...You can process it through journaling, through a negative and positive letter. The negative helps you get it out of your system. The positive reminds you of the things you love about the other party. Then you can go deal with them over the issue in a balanced way.

YOUR POSITIVE LETTERS

Now what do you do with your positive letters? You have three options. First, for letters involving people, if those people are alive and sharing would be a healthy situation, you can share the letters with them. But remember, there are times when even a positive letter can open a Pandora's Box. Especially when it comes to old relationships. You might be working on making amends and settling things, but the other party might not be ready for that. And that's OK, they don't have to be. The important thing is that you do it for you so you can heal things inside of yourself.

Second, if a person who is the subject of a letter is dead, you can go to the cemetery, visit their grave, maybe bring them some flowers, and read the letter to them. This is a very therapeutic, very powerful exercise.

Third, you can use your positive letters as affirmation letters, as I already mentioned. Use them as something you can refer back to, to realize and appreciate all of the positive things in your life and all of the positive things you are learning through recovery.

The bottom line is that it is extremely important that we use this process for growth and healing. In the Twelve Step Program, this is covered in the Fourth Step, which describes the process as taking "a fearless moral inventory." You don't do an inventory to make yourself sicker. You do it to make yourself healthy.

In Summary

The whole idea of journaling, of doing your inventory—positive and negative—helps you learn your personal history. So many of us would like to forget parts of our histories, or discard them outright. We can't do that. All that you can do is embrace your history. And then learn from it. Learn what it teaches you about yourself. About why you act the way you act, why you are attracted to certain types of people and relationships—even when they are not healthy for you. Learn about the things that you just have to accept and let go, and what things, what issues, you need to work on yet.

But I want to say yet again...Do not attempt journaling or your other Family of Origin work until you have completed the first four steps of recovery, until you have stabilized your situation, especially any addictions or other codependent behaviors. Otherwise, you might resurrect feelings that will only activate these behaviors, and whatever family work you've done to that point you will only have to do over again. I see this all the time, in hospitals, in rehabs, in therapy groups. People try to do too much family work too soon, and it only backfires. Sadly, in my experience, many psychiatrists and psychologists do not even understand this principle, do not understand the depth of the relationship between addiction relapse and premature Family of Origin work. When you activate issues when you are not prepared to face them, you also activate relapse into addictions and other negative behaviors.

My observation is that we want to dive right into our issues, our family work, because we want to eradicate the dysfunctionality in our lives, we want to settle all of our issues. Yet, as we said before, we will all have issues to work on fourteen days after we're dead, and dysfunctionality will always be with us. Dysfunctionality is part of life.

But once you go through the first four stages of recovery, and then into the fifth, you have a sound basis for the last, which we call Inner Child work. The rest of this book is about that work. It will cover some things you can do alone, and some that you should only do under the guidance of a professional therapist. I will get into a technique called Family Sculpture that helps you visualize what your Family of Origin was actually like, and I will get into a core concept, the concept of Shame—which is at the heart of many of our depressions and anxieties and other problems—and which is also something very different from Guilt. And I will try to demonstrate how Inner Child work, in healing the child within and developing the adult you now are, is something that we do as an ongoing process, the process of growth, of life.

Your Inner Child

THE FINAL STAGE OF THE RECOVERY PROCESS

As noted before, many of us codependents coming into treatment or recovery are in such emotional pain that we want to delve into our deep issues so we can get the quick "cure." And so much has been publicized about the "Inner Child" that we think the quickest way to our issues is to get in touch with the child within. But my own approach—I'll say it again—is that Inner Child work is the Sixth Stage—the final stage—of the recovery process. It must not be done until the other five—the *first* five—have been covered. Why? Because in getting in touch with your Inner Child you are naturally getting in touch with the part of your life in which you were a child, your past. And you simply don't know what you will find when you start delving into your past.

For example, we've all heard of cases of people who go into therapy and, after long months of work, suddenly remember trauma that they had repressed. We read the news stories about people who suddenly remember that they were sexually abused by an authority figure years before. Or people who suddenly recall long-forgotten episodes of incest, emotional abuse, physical abuse, abandonment...All sorts of issues and events. Sometimes the things remembered are such major traumas that we can't believe they actually happened, because we can't believe that they could possibly have been forgotten by the alleged victim. But repression—forgetting—is a basic defense mechanism of the human mind. If what we experienced was too overwhelming, too painful to accept, our minds simply block it out—until we are ready to face it again.

But even without major trauma, most, if not all, of us will uncover significant issues that developed over periods of time in our lives; for example, feelings of abandonment, neglect, and shame. In fact, many psychiatrists and psychologists think it might be easier to deal with major trauma than with more subtle forms of abuse. Think about it. The victim of major trauma, once the trauma is identified, knows that he or she was abused. Those of us victimized in more subtle ways, by chronic emotional abuse, for example, aren't as clearly aware of what our root problems are. In either case, we might have such powerful feelings about our issues that words like anger and frustration just aren't adequate to express what we feel. We discover that our Inner Child is full of *rage* and *bitterness*. We might also come to the realization that this is where our current depression and anxiety and addictions and other unhealthy behaviors stem from. When you reach that point, if you don't have a way of processing what you are discovering, you could very well become so embittered that you *become* your issues, as we discussed before. You get caught up in the Blame Game so much, are so driven by a desire for revenge against the people you think are responsible for your problems—your "victims," as we called them—that the issues become your whole life. Or you are driven to embalm yourself against the feelings you are resurrecting by falling back into your addictions: alcohol, drugs, sex, eating disorders, whatever.

You also have to remember that what you "uncover" in delving into your Inner Child are your *perceptions.* Even though these perceptions are real enough to you, are holding you in your current codependency, they might not, in fact, be completely accurate. Which again is why you need a healthy environment in which to process your perceptions.

It all goes back to the basic principle: the only reason you get in touch with your Inner Child issues is *to learn* from them. The only way you can learn from them is, first, to feel the feelings that come along with them. Which means that you cannot fall back into your addictions, which are merely ways of avoiding your feelings. Second, to learn from your issues, you must be able to sort them out, to process them, in a healthy environment. You get the healthy environment and the protection from relapsing into addictions through the first five stages of the recovery process. Then, and only then, are you ready for Inner Child work.

A SIMPLE DEFINITION OF INNER CHILD

You might find the following definition of Inner Child to be helpful in this stage of recovery. Think of your Inner Child as the emotional part of you, as opposed to your intellectual part, which may be referred to as the Adult you. One is not "good" and the other "bad." The idea is to bring them into balance. You'll see this definition in more detail as we get deeper into the Inner Child stage.

GETTING IN TOUCH

Getting in touch with, or exploring, your Inner Child is often referred to as Relapse Prevention Work. It helps identify your codependent patterns and where they came from in your childhood, and it prepares you to face the feelings you are resurrecting by exploring your past without escaping into your addictions. It prepares you to deal with your patterns, issues, and feelings.

There are several ways you can proceed with Inner Child work. Some of them we already mentioned: individual therapy; group therapy; the Twelve Step program, particularly inventorying or journaling. Usually we use a combination of methods. As one therapist describes it, each method is like going over the same ground, but with a different tool for a different effect. What I would like to do at this point is describe two other methods, the Geneogram and the Family Sculpture. They come with a warning. They are not for amateurs; you don't learn a little about them and then go off and do them alone or with friends. You do them under the guidance of a trained therapist or counselor.

All of the methods will teach you a lot about yourself, but the key lessons will be the patterns you picked up in the earliest stages of your life and the fact that those patterns *are still affecting you today!* I'll give you an example in a moment, but first I want to go back to one of the codependent diseases: the *I Know* disease. You see, at this point, some of you are saying "I know, I know. I know what happened in my childhood. I don't have to look at it again. What's the point?" The point is that knowing alone doesn't help you. If it did, you wouldn't be reading this book. You wouldn't be suffering from codependency and the depression and anxiety and addictions that come with it. If you want to get emotionally healthy and experience the serenity and happiness that goes with that, you have to *work* with your self-knowledge. Use it for something. Which is what this Sixth Stage is all about.

The example I'll share with you is very simple. It involves a young woman who recently got married. Now that the honeymoon part of the relationship is over, she finds that she doesn't trust her husband, and she often gets very angry at him. Yet he really hasn't done anything she can identify as the cause of her resentment. When the problem gets bad enough and she begins working on it in therapy, she discovers that in her family history, her personal history, her father and brothers and other men in her early life either abandoned her or hurt her in some way. Maybe they were there for her physically, but not emotionally. For her, that became a "normal," a pattern she expects to be repeated. So now, years later, she is taking out her anger and resentment on her husband, expecting him to hurt her, too, and reacting to it *in advance*. That's the Inner Child. The emotional part of us. The angry, frustrated part. When it's out of balance.

To get the Inner Child back into balance with the Inner Adult, the rational part of us, we use the methods described above. Again, to focus on the two, the Geneogram will give you a visual presentation of certain recurrent issues on paper, while the Family Sculpture gives it in three dimensions.

THE GENEOGRAM

The Geneogram is a family history diagram. To compose one, you would sit down with a trained counselor and basically construct a family tree, focusing on recurring issues for as far back as you could go. Some people who do this get a powerful awakening, a realization that many of the same issues recur in their families for generations, like alcohol abuse, abandonment, physical abuse, emotional abuse, and so on. Take the case of a young child who ends up in foster care because of certain neglect and abuse issues. His biological father is not in the picture; he left the marriage, abandoning wife and child, shortly after the child was born. The mother has substance abuse issues and was attracted to a live-in boyfriend who then abused both her and the child.

Remarkably, when a Geneogram was constructed for the child, it was discovered that the same patterns had been repeated in the mother's family for as far back as the local social agency had records. For example, the grandmother had ongoing substance abuse issues. She, too, had been abandoned by her husband after childbirth. And it was likely that the same pattern had occurred with the great-grandmother as well. In short, the family had been actively involved with the same issues and same agency involvement for generations.

The purpose of constructing the Geneogram in this case is to focus the efforts of counselors, and later of the child himself as he gets into therapy, on the particular issues that recur with this family. It is *one* tool that can be used with many others in the child's eventual recovery process, which would probably not begin to take effect until the child grew into an adult who could understand the events in his life.

THE FAMILY SCULPTURE

In my lectures, when the series is well advanced into discussing recovery, I often use the example of the Family Sculpture to show how a personal history can be presented in three dimensions. The example takes about an hour. But I stress to the class that the Family Sculpture process, done as part of counseling, can take two or three years. It should also be done as part of a group process, since, as you will see, people—actual bodies—are used to depict significant people and issues in the subject's life.

The process starts with the subject providing as complete a family history as possible to a counselor, who then identifies the people and issues to be depicted, and in what manner they are to appear. The end result is like a living tableau that shows the subject a portion of his or her life in three-dimensional detail. As with a Geneogram, *seeing* things this way often evokes a powerful realization in the subject.

As an example, I'll use a composite case from one of my own groups. For the subject person, a woman, we needed people from the group to play the roles of her father, mother, brother, and sister. Hers was a relatively small family; some sculptures are populated by grandparents, aunts, uncles, friends, teachers—whatever people were significant to the subject for the period being depicted. From her personal history, the written inventory the woman did for the period of her life being depicted, we also identified her church, shame, guilt, abuse, addiction, isolation, anger, and resentment as major issues, so she chose group members to portray each of those as well.

Now, the situation with the example subject was that when she was a child she did not have healthy, nurturing relationship with her mother. Instead, her mother virtually "smothered" her, was afraid to let the woman even go out and play with other children. So in the sculpture, we had the woman lie down on her back while the person playing the role of her mother was asked to sit on a chair that straddled the woman's legs. The significance is that the woman never really experienced a complete separation, a complete "birth," from the mother's womb. In the sculpture it is as though she is still half in the womb—and only half out of it. She essentially lived for the mother, and vice versa.

As for the father, he never really had a close relationship with the mother. He was one of those many fathers who, after having children, abdicated any emotional responsibility to the marriage. So the person playing him in the sculpture was placed with his back to the mother, looking away. Essentially he was there, but not there. He had very little contact with the woman.

The people playing the brother and sister were placed standing on either side of the mother, but also, like the father, with their backs to her—and to each other. Basically, except for the smothering that the mother gave the subject, there was no real closeness in the family when the subject was a child.

At this point, we stand back and look at the sculpture. We actually get the subject off the floor and ask her to step back and look at things, while we get a surrogate to play her in the sculpture. What does she see? She sees some myths that she's been living with, some "sacreds" that she is going to have to let go of. For example, when she looks at old family photographs, they don't look at all like the sculpture she's now seeing. They are all posed with everyone smiling and standing together, everyone close and happy. But the sculpture, taken from the words of her own history, doesn't paint such a rosy picture. There was no healthy closeness in this family. No intimacy. Yet—generally—all her life, the subject thought of her family as emotionally healthy and nurturing. Weren't all families? And hers was as good as any she had known.

With that attitude, when the subject experienced problems related to the family, she wound up concluding that there was something wrong with *her,* not with the family. She *shamed* herself. After all, if she believed that there was no dysfunction in her family, it had to be in her. But now, seeing her family portrayed, she's starting to see something different.

But we go on with the sculpture. We ask the woman to exchange places with her surrogate again, to actually lie down on her back on the floor, half covered by the person playing the role of her mother. It's interesting that at that point, returning to the situation, she comments on how she feels crowded and confined and stifled in the position she's in. But she hasn't really seen anything yet. Her church was a big part of her early life. If her mother didn't have any passion for her husband and family, she certainly had it for their church. The mother did everything she could for the church—went to as many services as she could, did volunteer work, even cleaned the parish building—and she took her daughter, our subject, along with her as much as she could. So, in the sculpture, the person chosen to play the church is placed standing on a chair—a symbolic pedestal—above the head of the entire family. From her mother, our subject learned to do for the church—and do and do and continue doing—never even taking a break to satisfy the normal wants and needs of a growing girl, not even a need as simple as playing with friends.

As a result, our subject's issues begin to develop around her—which is where we place each person from her group chosen to portray the individual issues. For example, she experienced deep anger and resentment from an early age. In fact, in therapy, it was suggested to her that she probably suffered from depression—*clinical* depression, not just normal feelings of sadness—from the time she was two or three years old. Imagine that. Being depressed *all your life*. But I'm sure many of us *can* imagine that. Many of us have experienced it.

Addiction became an issue for our subject because her father was an alcoholic. A functional alcoholic. He made work most days, but otherwise embalmed himself with alcohol, so he was present in the family physically, but unavailable for a healthy relationship. And the mother was an addict. A food addict. Worse, not only did she have the problem, she also encouraged her daughter to adopt it. When the daughter felt sad, the mother would give her messages like, "Eat, you'll feel better." And so the subject began to develop a food addiction that grew with her, literally, into adult life.

We continue building our subject's sculpture by placing her other issues strategically around her—though I'm saving her *major* issue—the major issue of all codependents—for last. Her guilt came into play in a very subtle way because of the anger and resentment she had for her family, particularly her parents. Family, after all, is one of the "sacreds" in life. And parents are among the most "sacred" of the "sacreds." When you challenge a sacred, or even feel anything negative about it, you experience guilt.

She also experienced a not-so-subtle guilt. Her mother's idea of a religious education was to emphasize guilt. The messages were something like: God is a wrathful, angry God; you deserve to be punished; obey your parents and church and all authority figures without question; your body is sinful...And so on. Many of us are familiar with them. We experienced at least some of them ourselves.

The more the guilt and anger and resentment crowded around our subject in life—as they are crowded around her in the sculpturing process—the more isolated and abandoned she felt. And the emotional neglect she experienced was tantamount to abuse. If that concept of abuse is difficult for you to accept, consider that it is a medical fact that neglected children often experience stunted physical growth—aside from the damage done to their psyche.

We complete our subject's sculpture by symbolically placing what becomes the *Major Issue* for codependents right above her, straddling her chest over her heart. Everything negative she experienced went into developing this issue. She felt it, as we said, when she felt her anger and resentment at the "sacreds" in her life. She felt it more when she found herself becoming more and more isolated. And it grew even more as her food addiction and weight problem made her feel more and more physically different. Basically, she started feeling like there was something wrong with her. That became her normal. And that feeling is called **Shame.**

In my own sculpture, my therapist played out the psychodrama not only with people playing roles, but also by layering blankets on me to show just how stifled and smothered I was by my issues. As with the subject as we described the process above, I was invited to step out of the sculpture and look at it. Then it was photographed and videotaped and I was given the films. I can look at them from time to time to help me visualize my issues and patterns, particularly as they relate to my Inner Child. I found it to be a very powerful experience. And many of those in my groups describe it the same way.

But this is only the first part of the sculpting process. We continue with it and lead into a major goal of all of our recovery work: Shame Reduction.

REMAKING THE SCULPTURE

The sculpting process is a psychodrama. So to get the most out of it, to finish the drama, so to speak, you want to play out the sculpture, take the scene into one of recovery. For our subject, recovery meant getting in touch with her feelings through individual and group therapy, journaling, and other methods. By working her individual program, she was able to discover that she actually did have feelings of guilt and resentment toward her family. What she had to do was acknowledge those feelings and then decide what she wanted to do with them. Her decision was that she would no longer deny the feelings, but keep them as part of her life, her history, so she could actually learn from them by referring back to them from time to time. In the sculpture, this is represented by moving the figures of guilt and resentment off to the side. They are available for our subject to examine when she wants, but they are no longer helping to suffocate her or hold her down.

The same thing happens with guilt. She acknowledges it, but places it aside where it can be examined as she progresses through her individual program. It's extremely helpful to remember two things when dealing with guilt. First, it's part of life. It doesn't go away. Which is why, in the sculpture, it's placed aside, not eliminated. Guilt will poke its head into life from time to time. And it can be a good thing. We should feel guilty when we do something unhealthy or harmful to ourselves or others. But the second thing to remember about guilt is that it has to be kept in balance. Accept responsibility for your actions. Then make amends where and when you can. Then let go of the guilt.

In our subject's case, in her sculpture, her guilt was inappropriate. She had every right to feel her anger and resentment. So the figure of her guilt, though not eliminated, because it is still an issue with her, is placed very far off to the side.

To skip a little in this example, in the finished sculpture, the subject's family is removed from around her and moved off just a bit. This part of the sculpture represents the transition in her life that she is no longer half in her mother's womb; she does not live for her mother. She makes her own choices. And her family generally is around her; she can call them into her life as she chooses.

In fact, the subject's father is dead. But he remains in the picture, the sculpture, of her life, because she still has a very real relationship with him. She has the anger and resentment of his not having been there for her emotionally when she was a child. But she has come to accept him with those flaws and loves him as he was, as she knew him. We'll get back to that, but let's deal with the church and shame and addiction in the example.

Both the church and shame are taken down from their pedestals. In real life, the subject still has a relationship with her church, but she has come to believe that it is not the monolith she thought it was; she no longer looks to it to dictate every move in her life. So it is placed off to the side, just behind her family. She can interact with her church as she chooses, bring it closer when she chooses.

Shame can be removed—almost, but not quite, eliminated. The more she deals with it, the more she realizes how inappropriate her shame feelings are. There is *nothing* fundamentally wrong with her. So we place shame even beyond her other issues, something to be acknowledged and learned from, but kept at a healthy distance.

Now, addiction in the sculpture is being moved out on its own. It, too, will not go away. It will always be something our subject has to face, particularly her food addiction. Its placement is symbolic in that it has to be put under arrest. Our subject acknowledges that she is an addict. Addiction remains in her life, and so in her sculpture. It continues to remain even though she's made tremendous progress in real life in developing healthy eating habits. She has to remember that stress can bring on her addiction again, so she keeps it under arrest.

Now there is nothing holding our subject down, except inertia. So we can move her in the sculpture, bring her up from under the chairs and off her back and let her stand at the center of her own life. And we get back to her family. She faces them, including her deceased father. The symbolism is that she accepts them for who they are. She can deal with them directly. She can reach out and bring them into her life as she chooses. Her contact with her father, of course, is spiritual, mental. It takes a form that she defines. For example, in my own life, my father died when I was just twenty-six. I had ambivalent feelings toward him, just as our subject has for her father. But I came to accept my father for who he was, and I pray to him and meditate on him from time to time. As a result, I came to understand him more. So I learn from him and grow through him even now.

VISUALIZATION

As I said when we started with the example sculpture, I simply wanted to give you an idea of what the process is like. In the example, we had to smooth over several things that would have been examined in much more detail in an actual sculpting exercise. And please remember that an actual exercise can develop over months and years. It is the culmination—not the beginning—of a long phase of your personal recovery program. That phase includes, as we said before, writing out your history; having it analyzed; and having the sculpture done under the guidance of a trained counselor or therapist.

The value of sculpting is visualization. I have had many, many people in my groups tell me that they were helped tremendously in doing their Inner Child work when they actually *saw* a phase of their lives laid out in three dimensions, especially since, in group, we discuss the sculpture as we construct it. To sum up, I would say that in the sculpting process you get to

1. See your Inner Child as it developed at a critical phase in your early life;
2. Embrace your personal history;
3. Build a relationship between the adult you and your Inner Child so you can now parent yourself; and
4. Make amends with the past and move on.

When you delve into your Inner Child deep enough to construct a model of it, you delve into every part of your life and of your family's life, as much as you can remember. When you do that, you're going to see not only where your own present issues stem from, but how they were issues for your parents as well—part of your Geneogram. And, if you are like most people who have gone through the process, you will eventually come to the realization that dysfunctionality really is OK, just a part of life. It is something to learn from to make life better. When you get to that point, you are well on your way to tackling the issue I'd like to get back to now.

11

Shame

THE SHAME PROCESS

As you get more into your recovery, you will realize that the major issue of codependents is shame. Understand what shame is. It is the belief that there is something wrong with you. Contrast this to guilt, in which the essential element is the belief that you *did* something wrong. There is a huge difference in *your actions* being wrong, or unhealthy, and the belief that *you* are somehow defective, right down to your core. When you do something you know you shouldn't have done, you can correct your behavior. But when you believe that you are fundamentally flawed, how do you correct that? And once you come to believe that there is something wrong with you, doesn't it seem only logical that depression, anxiety, and all sorts of other codependent symptoms will follow? For example, you will find yourself in unhealthy relationships, trying to get the approval and approbation of another person, just so you can feel good about yourself, no matter what the relationship costs you. Or you will find yourself caught up in addiction trying to embalm the chronic bad feeling that is deep in your heart and gut.

From my own experience, I would say that shame is the major issue in 95% of everything that happens in our lives. Second, shame is an issue that involves power, ownership, and boundaries—which is where I will focus on addressing methods of shame reduction. Notice I say "reduction," not elimination. You cannot eliminate shame in life. From the time of birth, we participate in what I call the Shame Process, a normal, if certainly not pleasant, part of life. There's an old saying that if you put two human beings together in the same room, you will eventually have shame issues. Why? Because we are human. Shame, like dysfunctionality, is part of the human condition. In recovery, we attempt to learn from our shame issues and reduce them to where they no longer plague us. Otherwise, the ongoing feeling of shame we carry traumatizes and paralyzes us, though most of us don't appreciate the depth of the problem.

Our shame comes from two places: Original Shame and Traumatic Shame. When they build on each other until they become like a critical mass, they become Toxic Shame, causing all sorts of problems in our lives.

ORIGINAL SHAME

Original Shame messages are usually subtle, especially because they happen to you as a child. They tell you *indirectly* that there's something wrong with you. For example, you want to go out and play with Johnny, but your mom tells you not to hang around with him. The unspoken message is that there's something wrong with you for not picking better friends and not realizing on your own that there's something wrong with the ones you have. Or you ask your dad to read a story to you, but he says no. He doesn't explain that he's tired, so you get the message that there's something wrong with your asking. You feel shamed, whether you know it or not. Other subtle shame messages come in the form of telling you not to go out and play because you might get hurt, or basically not to do other normal things because somebody just doesn't like it. They are subtle because they are not necessarily intended to make you feel bad. They might even be given with the best intentions, because the person telling them to you actually believes that the normal things you want are bad for you. All of us have had such messages from the first authority figures in our lives. Which is why we say they are part of life, inevitable. The problem is that we receive a steady stream of them as we grow older, and they eventually make us feel that there is something wrong with us. We become what psychologists call "Shame Based." Shame becomes our normal.

TRAUMATIC SHAME

This, simply, is shame that comes from certain events in your life. For example, a sexually abused child is a shamed child. Deprivation and poverty can be long-term "events" that generate shame. One of the events that many people describe is always being the last to be chosen in a game when they were children, or the one who never had a date in high school. All of these generate shame, to a greater or lesser degree, but enough so that the feeling of shame certainly sinks in.

EXPECTATIONS

To further explore both forms of shame, let's look at the core of shame itself: Expectation. When we are born, and as we are little children growing up, we have expectations. You expect your family—whatever your Family of Origin is—to love you, like you, feed you, clothe you, nurture you, teach you...All normal and natural expectations. They are also very concrete expectations. When my family doesn't meet my expectations, I feel shamed. For example, you want to experience unconditional love from your family, but there are days when they make you feel like you were a mistake, when they wish you had never been born. Some parents, in anger, actually tell their children this from time to time. So instead of receiving unconditional love, I'm being abandoned and emotionally abused and receiving all sorts of other negative messages.

I said we play the Shame Game. The game happens when it's played in different dimensions, so to speak. You see, the family also has expectations of you. Like, children should be seen but not heard; they expect you to be quiet when they want you to be quiet. They put that demand on you. You see, in reality, expectations are demands.

Your family also expects—demands—what? Ask different people and hear what demands were put on them: to always get good grades, to become a doctor, or to take over the family business, or always mind your manners. Expectations. Demands. And when you don't meet them, the family lets you know you let them down, there's something wrong with you—maybe even that they are *ashamed* of you.

Now, for those of you falling into the I Know game at this point, I want to assure you that I also know. I know that the family had its expectations of me and made its demands on me for reasons. They wanted me to survive, and thrive, and be polite, and be accepted, and all sorts of other good things. But, despite the intentions of those making demands on me, the process still resulted in shame. And the Shame Game expanded as we grew older. As we had more contact with our environment, we realized that our neighbors had expectations of us. Our religious systems had expectations of us. If we didn't meet the first, we would not be accepted. We would be ostracized. If we didn't meet the second, God would surely punish us. I would be branded as bad.

One person I know was born through caesarean section. Her mother almost died in the process. As a child, she had an aunt who would watch her sometimes while her mother was at work. Whenever the child misbehaved, the aunt had a way of controlling her. She would scold the child, "You almost killed your mother once. Do you want to kill her now with your misbehavior!?" She was only four or five years old and had that indictment laid on her, that she almost *killed her own mother!* To understand the impact of something like that, and of all shame messages, consider life through the eyes of a child. A child doesn't think in terms of adult logic. The child doesn't say, "Oh, yeah, auntie. I understand. You're just saying that because you need to calm me down." Children don't function that way. A child functions in a child's mind, an emotional mind. So whatever the adult says, the child believes. To the child, it's almost as though God is saying it.

To the child, what the adult says becomes what is supposed to be, becomes the child's normal.

If you want to get a feel for this, stand over the crib of a baby and try to imagine what that infant sees. To the infant, you are mammoth, a giant. As far as the child is concerned, *you* are the Higher Power. Whatever you say becomes reality for the child.

It's sad sometimes, but we adults play all kinds of expectation games, shame games, with children—without even knowing the impact we are having. I remember once going into a restaurant with my wife. A man came in with his two-year-old son. He had the boy placed in a high chair and then proceeded—and I love this—to talk him about how he should behave in a restaurant. "Don't make any noise. Don't play with your food. Mind your manners." It took all of about five minutes for the kid to dump something on the floor. And the father started screaming, "Didn't I just tell you...!" The shame game. The kid just did something totally natural for a two year old, and the father is yelling at him. In public no less. The child gets a shame message: I must be bad. Keep doing that to the kid and eventually you'll see him with one of those tatoos: Born to be bad. The message will have sunk in.

Now think about this...We also said that society, the neighborhood, peers, religion—all put other expectations on us. Here's the scary part. Some of those expectations clash. Your family insists that you *always* behave the way they want. Your friends insist on something else. Or your family raises you in their religious tradition and expects you to follow it to the letter. But they don't practice what they preach. Confusing? How does a child cope? How did *we* cope? We became good little codependents. When we were with our family, we followed the family's rules. When we were with our friends, we followed their rules. We became little chameleons. And we felt guilty about it. We felt as though we were violating one group or the other, and that made us feel bad about ourselves—whether or not we knew it. The feeling was there. The feeling is shame.

So later in life, shame becomes our mask. Under it are the other issues: guilt, fear, abuse, abandonment, dependency...

COMPOUND SHAME

So there we are leaving childhood with our mask and the issues it's hiding, and what happens to us? We have *more* expectations dumped on us. For example, I get a job, the job has expectations of me. If I don't live up to them, I get scared. I might get fired. And I get into a relationship and that comes with expectations. As a codependent, I probably get into a relationship with someone who has expectations like, "If you really love me, then you will do this." The "this" is basically clean up my mess for me or act in a way that lets me keep playing my own codependent role. So as children, we have our Original Shame and Traumatic Shame and we know how to play the Shame Game and we carry it all into adulthood. All the systems we get into come with expectations. All have the potential to shame us. And we're conditioned toward shame.

Even in recovery we play the shame game. We put expectations on ourselves: have to make so much progress in so much time, or else I failed. And others put expectations on us. I've seen sponsors in AA programs tell people that they have to work that program just such a way or the sponsors will quit working with them. So what happens? The person slips up a bit and they learn a new game: deception. Tell the sponsor what he wants to hear. The white lie. Which also creates shame. And adds to the addiction itself.

Codependents are good at deception. Why not? We learned it when trying to balance the expectations of our families against those of our peers when we were kids. And we continued learning it as we entered other systems. So we do it even in recovery, in therapy, in working whatever program we get into.

THE SHAME WARS

I call this whole process of compounding shame. The Shame Wars. I have expectations of you and everybody else, and you and everybody else—every system I participate in—have expectations of me. For example, as mentioned before, we get into recovery and all of a sudden want our families to participate. We *expect* them to participate, to *want to* participate. After all, we have suddenly found the Truth, the reason for all of our family problems. All they have to do is get with it and all our dysfunctionality will be gone, we will heal, and we will all live happily ever after as the perfect family. By approaching the family this way, all you are doing is shaming them, telling them what's *wrong* with them. As a result, they react by shaming you, by countering with what's wrong with you and the things in the past that you did wrong. The Shame Game. The Shame Wars. To put it in Twelve Step terms, you are trying to do their inventory for them, and they defend themselves by trying to do your inventory for you. You are shaming one another. You are, in simple terms, beating one another up.

I look at my own experience. I can joke about it now. When I was a cleric, I didn't like all of the Church's rules. I knew I could never be happy living by them, so I went around trying to get the Church to change for me. What I was saying, in effect, was, "I have these expectations of you. You have to meet them. You have to change so I can be happy." It was easier for me to try to change the Church than to change myself.

If that sounds crazy, think about it for a minute. How many of us do the same thing? "If only my family would change..." "If only my job would change..." "If only my friends would change..." And on and on. Now, if we all expect everything to change for us, guess what? We have a major problem. It's called chaos. Because the changes we all want don't jibe. So in the end we are all going to be disappointed all over again. We are going to be shamed. And when the Shame Wars start, we get into the victim game, blaming everybody else for what's wrong in our own lives. "I drink because of you." "I use drugs because of you." "You made my childhood miserable, so my adulthood is miserable because of you."

If you want to see this in a microcosm, look at a classic codependent relationship: the alcoholic and his/her spouse. Alcoholics play the shame game because they want their spouses to understand their drinking and clean up their mess for them. The spouses, on the other hand, get to call the alcoholics bums every time they come home drunk, get to blame the alcoholic for every-thing wrong in life.

But let me flesh this out for you. I heard a call once on talk radio, a psychologist's call-in show. A woman called and said she had a problem: her husband was sick. He was an alcoholic. She said that for *nine years* she had been waiting for him to change, to just do something simple, like take her and the kids on a Sunday picnic. But every Saturday he would get drunk and wake up Sunday sick and hung over. He had neither the interest nor the ability to take them on a picnic—for *nine years. The* psychol-ogist told the woman the truth: she was the sick one. He told her, if you want to go on a picnic with the kids, get up and go. Stop blaming the husband for making your life miserable because he's a drunk and won't take you on a picnic. Of course, if she did that, she'd have to get into other issues with her marriage and how miserable she was in that situation. And she might have to make a choice: change it or continue to live in misery. And a change that big is scary. So she was marking time for nine years by basi-cally playing the shame game with her alcoholic husband.

To get back to my own example with the Church, I remember getting to the point where I complained more and more. *If only the Church would change...*And one day my therapist said, "Vince, did you ever stop to think that this might be *your* issue. I mean, the Church is pretty clear on it: *Here's the rule. If you don't like it, you change.* And he was right. Dead right. It was so clear. The Church had laid out its rules in black and white hun-dreds of years ago. Yet I was running around saying, "Me change? No, you change!"

We see it in all relationships and all situations. When prob-lems come along, things we don't like, we have a tendency to get into a shame exchange, an insanity exchange, the Shame Wars. *Everything would be all right with me if only you would change.* It's so common, because, as we said before, shame is part of life. It is normal. The trick is to learn a technique that we are going to get into a little later: shame reduction. If we don't, our shame truly becomes toxic.

TOXIC SHAME

I'd like to give you an equation:

ORIGINAL SHAME + COMPOUNDED SHAME = TOXIC SHAME

In other words, if you don't learn shame reduction, shame will grow until it ruins your life with depression, anxiety, addictions...with codependency—and all the signs and symptoms that come with it.

I already gave you an example of someone living in toxic shame, the alcoholic's wife who called into that radio station. Let me give you another. It involves a woman I know who was sexually abused by her father when she was a child. She went through six marriages. *Six.* And when she was finally in her 60's she was able to talk to me about it. She had finally come to understand that

1. She harbored a furious rage against her father;
2. That rage had created a terrible sense of shame in her; and
3. The shame had become toxic until she actually *became* her own issues—lived those issues every day of her life.

When she was three, she had the natural expectations we all have of our fathers. When he didn't meet them, she transferred those expectations onto six husbands. And when they couldn't meet them she beat the hell out of them and finally left them, one by one. And it wasn't until she was in her 60's that she realized that the issue was HERS.

Was her father right? NO! Was she hurt and traumatized? Yes. But, FOR WHATEVER REASON, she had not dealt with the shame and so it grew and compounded until she became the shame, which she then projected onto SIX husbands.

TOXIC PEOPLE, PLACES, AND THINGS

I'd like to share two stories with you. The first is about two people relocating to a new town. To get to the town, they had to cross a bridge where an old toll taker worked. As the first person drove up to the toll booth, she told the man that she was relocating to the town and asked what it was like. "Well," he said, "if you don't mind my asking, what was your old town like?" "Well," she said, "it was actually pleasant. Nice people. Friendly. Like family." The old man smiled and told her, "Then you should like this place. It's just like that." The woman passed on and the next driver pulled up. She, too, told the toll man she was relocating and asked what the town was like. He asked her the same question about her old town. "It was nasty," she said. "Couldn't get along with the people. Very unfriendly. Very cold." The old man shook his head. "Sorry to tell you," he said. "But I'm afraid that's just what you'll find here."

The second story is similar. It comes from eastern tradition. It has to do with a man who went on a trip through the forest. Towards evening, as he was getting tired, he thought to himself, "Wouldn't it be nice to find a nice grassy knoll where I could sleep tonight?" Sure enough, around the next bend, he saw just such a knoll. "Wouldn't it be nice if there was a stream nearby so I could wash and get a cool drink?" Sure enough, he heard the gurgling of water and saw a stream just through the woods. Just as he was bedding down for the night he reflected, "That was strange. First I wish for a knoll and it appears. Then I wish for a stream and find one. This place is spooky. I wonder if there are any ghosts here?" And guess what he saw?

I think you get the point. Sometimes we create our own reality. And sometimes we get caught up in the negative so much that we create a negative reality for ourselves. When I explain this in terms of shame, I use the analogy of people, places, and things becoming toxic to us. The more we associate with them, the more shamed we get, the more we create our own negativity.

For example, I meet so many people in my practice who have issues with their parents. Instead of looking at their childhoods, learning from them, and moving on, they create their parents as victims or scapegoats. We touched on it before: "I am depressed because of what you did to me when I was a child" or "I am an addict because of you" or "I am dysfunctional because of you." Then they add, "If only you would have changed..." Or "If only you would change now..." So guess what these people find when they get together with their parents, or, in the case of parents who are dead, with the memory of them? They find shame. At toxic levels. They can't learn from the past, embrace it, accept it, and detach with love. They can't, as the Big Book of AA says, "Love them, pray for them, let them be who they are." So their parents remain toxic to them. And they remain toxic to their parents.

Another example...A couple I knew from rehab work. He was an alcoholic and she was a classic Caretaker. But their relationship was even more interesting than most codependent relationships. They had finally separated. So each day, after he had a bottle in his hand, he would call her. And they would yell and scream at each other on the phone. For *three or four hours! Each day!* Needless to say, they were toxic to each other. So the counselor told them to break it off, maybe even move to different states or something. They did. Then seven years later, he called again out of the blue. And they screamed and shouted at each other for three or four hours.

Or a final example...Another man in rehab. When he was in his active addiction, he would get drunk and drive down a certain street in his truck firing a pistol in the air like a cowboy. He got arrested a few times, lost a few pistols, got into a lot of stuff. Today, he's fifteen years sober and cannot go down that street. He just gets scared to death—clinically it's called Anxiety—when he even goes near the place.

In short, toxic people, places, and things are those that activate shame feelings in you. The guy at work who holds a grudge for something you did years ago is toxic to you. You are toxic to someone else when you are the grudge holder. A bar is toxic to an alcoholic. Your past can be toxic. Anything you do not learn from and make peace with becomes toxic. That's just a fact of life—even though we are just learning it.

And you can carry your toxic patterns into your present. For example, I go to the airport to leave on vacation, but I find out that my plane will be an hour late. So many of us in this situation will get all bent out of shape, curse the airline, curse the counter people, shame them—and shame ourselves in the process. But the fact is, the plane's late. It happens. Yet this simple event becomes the trigger to activate my shame patterns; I take it all personally. I create insanity around it. And it's all very needless. Which leaves us with a choice. We can continue to victimize ourselves with our old codependent, shame patterns. Or we can learn to change them, tackle Shame as our CORE ISSUE, head-on.

MEANS OF CHANGE

Earlier I said that I like the Twelve Step approach for dealing with codependent issues, and I'd like to elaborate why. The approach came from the AA movement that began in the 1930's. By the 1970's, psychologists and psychiatrists were learning that the approach could be applied to a wide range of problems, not just substance addictions. Basically the Twelve Steps lead you to

1. Admitting the problem, whatever it is;
2. Developing an awareness of the extent of the problem; and
3. Giving you something *to do* to address the problem.

I cannot emphasize the third point enough. If you have experience with therapy, you might also have experienced the problem that many of us who have tried therapy alone have encountered: we get all this self-knowledge, but we don't know what to do with it. We go into therapy because of depression, anxiety, and/or addictions and all sorts of other codependent behaviors and symptoms, but we find that the knowledge we gain doesn't do much on its own to alleviate our problems. The Twelve Steps tell us what to do with our hard-earned self-knowledge. And they have another tremendous advantage as well: they address Shame head-on.

One of the best books dealing with shame is the Big Book of AA. I recommend it, even if alcohol isn't a problem of yours. As the Twelve Steps have been applied to many problems, so the Big Book of the first Twelve Step program can be applied to a broad range of problems.

From the Twelve Step methodology, the Big Book, and all the other approaches we spoke of—individual therapy, group work, inventorying, etc.—you will hear two basic principles. First, every time you get stuck blaming somebody else for your present situation—the Blame Game—all you are doing is avoiding your own issues. Yes, maybe they did you wrong, serious wrong. But you are in the present now. Are you going to face your experience, learn from it, and move on? Or are you going to stay stuck? Second, there are three things you will need to learn and absorb in order to deal with shame. They are sometimes called the Big Three: Boundaries, Acceptance, Love.

Now notice. I have not used the words "eliminate" or "get rid of" or anything like them in speaking about shame. I already said that shame and insanity and dysfunctionality are part of life—part of each of our lives, not just life in general. So when we speak of the Means of Change in regard to shame, when we talk about the Twelve Step approach, the Big Book, the Big Three, and all the other concepts we covered—as well as others we will cover in the final chapters—we are not talking about eliminating shame in our lives. We are talking about another concept, as introduced in the next chapter: Shame *Reduction.*

Shame
Reduction

USING ALL THE TOOLS

By now, I hope you can see that codependency is a complex problem. It is the manifestation of a number of issues, with the core issue of shame. Fortunately, while the problem may be complex, the solution is fairly straightforward. I would also say it is fairly simple, which is NOT to say that it is easy.

To recap, you can use a variety of methods to do your recovery work. You might get into individual therapy, move into group therapy, develop a Recovery Family, work the Twelve Steps, and so on. THERE IS NO HARD AND FAST FORMULA. THERE IS NO SET TIMETABLE. I hope that by now we have also made that much clear. You might try one method, get into others, get back to one, change to another, develop a twist or two of your own...But I think you will find that recovery does come down to the principles outlined in the Six Stages: awareness of yourself and your issues; a group that you can be intimate with in doing your work; actually doing the work by writing it out and talking it out, which are means of processing; and basically creating an environment that is secure enough for you to continue your work.

As you get into that work, you will come to recognize that core issue of codependency when you see it: shame. And you will learn how to reduce it. What I would like to get into in more detail here are the tools of shame reduction, starting with the Big Three: Boundaries, Acceptance, Love.

Boundaries

Setting boundaries for yourself is basically a process of creating your own space. Think of it like this. A country sets boundaries. If another country crosses those boundaries, it's considered an act of aggression, an invasion. So it is with you. When someone crosses your boundaries, they are invading your space. They do not have a right to do that. They do not have a right to cross your boundaries without permission.

Setting boundaries, to put it in terms we already discussed, is Self-Parenting, getting your own needs met. It is also developing the adult inside of you. I'd like to give a few examples.

I am an ex-clergyman. A while back I was invited to a celebration for a friend of mine, a clergyman who was celebrating his 25th year in the priesthood. I attended; the man is a good friend, our relationship positive and healthy. But at the affair, of course, were other clergymen, many of whom I knew, and some not on very positive terms. At the affair, I was told about a reunion celebration being planned for a group of clergymen, and I was invited. Later, at home, I was struggling with whether or not to accept the invitation. There would be a lot of people at the reunion with whom I had negative issues—and vice versa. For example, some took my leaving the priesthood as a put-down, as though I was saying that there was something wrong with the priesthood, and so something wrong with them for remaining priests—which is not what my leaving was about at all. In short, they were shamed by my action, and, if I were to meet them, they would undoubtedly want to argue it out, as they had done before with me, and so shame me. Basically, it would have been a who's right/who's wrong tug-of-war.

The child in me felt obligated. The Church was calling me again; the Church was a big, huge, power in my life as a child. Social obligations were calling me, and don't we have to be polite and accept invitations? And all sorts of other stuff was going on with my Inner Child.

But my adult was also active. For me to go to my friend's party was one thing, a positive thing, a real celebration of his priesthood. But for me to go to the reunion would only be negative, exposing myself—and some others there—to shame. So I set my boundaries. I didn't go to the reunion. Instead, when I received the written invitation, I sent back a nice thank you note with a declination. It was proper. It was polite. It was healthy for everybody concerned.

Another example...A person I knew who had just gotten into recovery had a dilemma. She was invited to a business affair. But she had an alcohol problem that she was just getting under control, and there would be drinking at the affair. Further, the "in-crowd" would expect her to join in the drinking and would get on her case if she didn't—especially the drunker they got. She didn't necessarily want them to know that she had finally decided she was an alcoholic in recovery. That might be used against her at work down the road. But she was in a recovery group that had sponsors, so she sat down with her sponsor and talked about it. The way these affairs went, there would be speakers during the first hour or so. Then the bar would open. About an hour later, it would all be in full swing.

With her sponsor, she settled on some boundaries. She would go the affair. Listen to the speakers. Then make the rounds saying hello to the old crowd, politely moving on from one to the next after a little small talk. Then leave without any fanfare. No big deal. A simple plan. A way to avoid toxic shame.

I dare say that if you are not used to setting boundaries, you are actually going to like it. Setting boundaries is: saying NO to unwanted advances, sexual or otherwise; discussing your personal life ONLY with people you feel safe with and ONLY when you feel like it; NOT BEING PRESSURED into doing something you really don't want to do. Get the swing of it? Think of a few examples yourself. I guarantee that the healthier you get, the easier it will be for you to set healthy boundaries. Also, the more adept you get at setting your own boundaries, the more YOU WILL RESPECT OTHER PEOPLE'S BOUNDARIES.

There is a little phrase we use in recovery about this aspect of shame reduction work: *The art and gift of setting boundaries is wisdom.*

ACCEPTANCE

This is a concept I will cover in more detail later, but it belongs here as well as part of the Big Three. I have a theory based on my own experience: *95% of all recovery, of all healthy living, is acceptance!*

The Big Three work hand-in-hand. First, you set boundaries, which clears a space around you, in a sense, to do your recovery work. Then, as you actually do the work, you start to come to a point of acceptance. Acceptance of what? Acceptance of the fact that you are dysfunctional; that your Family of Origin is dysfunctional; that the world is dysfunctional; that neither you, nor your family, or the world have to be perfect; that you do not have to control things, including other people, to get to perfection…Get the point? You start to accept things *as they are.* It's a beautiful concept, because then you let things flow, you don't try to force them. It takes a lot of pressure off you, lets you devote your energy to your own healthy recovery, instead of driving yourself crazy and beating yourself and others up trying to "cure" them. Keep a couple of things in mind when you think of acceptance.

First, just about every major philosophical movement in the world—religious or otherwise—preaches acceptance; they often call it detachment. Second, when you *accept* the fact that you cannot control other people, you can begin working on yourself. And, *when you work on yourself, everything else falls into place.*

With the Big Three concept, after you clear your space by setting boundaries and finally come to an acceptance that you are the only person you can work on, you will—probably slowly—begin to experience a sense of love.

LOVE

Let me tell you what love is not. It is not passion. It is not sex. It is not infatuation. And loving someone is not necessarily *liking* the way they are. Think about that last one. You can love someone and not like them.

In recovery, we refer to detaching from people, places, and things with love. It is a very difficult concept for most of us to understand. *It is something that you will experience gradually as you* **continue** *working on yourself.*

The problem is that we really do not understand love. For example, right now, as you read this, think of a person you think you love. What if that person stopped loving you in turn? Would you then stop loving them? If so, isn't that like a business transaction: *I'll love you if you love me back*?

Love is something that most of us have to work on. Not that you have to work on loving a person, place, or thing, or even yourself. We just have to relax and open ourselves up to what love really is. It is said that you can begin the process of loving someone by getting more knowledge of them. This applies to yourself as well; get to know yourself, and you will love yourself more.

Detaching with love is tricky. It takes some practice. Let me give you an example. I knew a woman once who detached from her husband. She did it by divorcing him and moving away. If you remember, we called this a geographical detachment. But she was still obsessed with him and all the wrongs she believed he had done her—and he had done some pretty nasty things. But there she was years after the divorce. She didn't even know where he was, if he was still alive. And she was still obsessed with him. So, in effect, she hadn't detached with love, but with anger. And so she really wasn't detached from him at all. It was like he was still living with her, still married. Still very much a part of her life.

On the flip side, let me share a personal experience. It actually has to do with my setting boundaries. After I left the priesthood, I had a friend whose wife was dying. He came to me and asked if I would give her the last rites, a sacrament in our Church. I told him that I couldn't do it. That was a boundary I had set. I had finally left the priesthood after a long struggle. I didn't want to revert back. I offered to get a priest friend of mine to give the rites, and I offered to come and pray with the dying woman. But that wouldn't do for my friend. When I stuck to my decision, he got angry at me. And he carried that anger against me till the day he died. But that was his issue. For my part, when he ended the friendship on his side, I still loved him. What he did hurt, but I accepted him and still loved him as a friend and person.

What is it that lets one person detach from a situation with love, while another person can only detach in obsessed anger? I personally think it has to do with a conscious understanding of grieving.

THE GRIEVING PROCESS

Grieving is another misunderstood concept. We know we grieve when someone dies or when someone close to us discovers that they have a serious illness. In short, we understand something of grieving when it involves losing a person or something major. But do you realize that you grieve every day? Do you realize that you grieve the loss of time, or even of something as subtle as an idea? We'll look at that, but first let's look at what has become known as the grieving process. It involves five steps: Denial, Bargaining, Anger, Depression, Acceptance. Here are a few examples of how it works.

Let's say you are driving somewhere and suddenly hear a strange noise coming from your car. I dare say your first reaction will be denial, something like, "Oh, it will go away." When it persists, you'll start bargaining: "It isn't serious" or "Well, I'll make it to where I'm going then have it looked into." When the car suddenly stops, you'll get angry; you know what you'll say then, I don't have to make up a quote. Then you'll get depressed: "Why me?" "Why now?" You might just hang your head on the steering wheel for a while. Then you'll come to acceptance: call a mechanic, deal with it.

I may as well say here that you probably won't do these steps in strict order, and that you'll probably skip back and forth among them, and that you might even do a few of them at the same time. Our minds and emotions are amazing; even as we're denying something, we're already accepting it.

In the above, when you get the car fixed and some time passes, it becomes something you really accept, maybe even laugh at, which means that you actually come to love it as part of your own experience.

Now look at a second example, a person faced with an unexpected divorce. First denial: "My spouse can't be serious. He/she is just upset. It will pass." When it doesn't pass, bargaining: approach the spouse and offer all sorts of promises in order to reconcile. When that doesn't work, anger: "Bastard/Bitch, I'll make him/her pay in court, get all I can out of this." Then depression: "I'm a failure, a loser." Then acceptance: "I may not even understand this at this point, but I have to accept it and move on." And, long after the divorce, maybe a melancholy night will come when the person's thinking reverts to "Maybe we can get together again." Or another time comes when the anger returns, or the depression. As we said, the steps play out in different rhythms and patterns for different people and circumstances.

Now let's look at a third situation, one more subtle. Let's look at ourselves as we get into recovery. We do our personal history and we realize: "My family is dysfunctional; I am dysfunctional." Trust me, you will go through the grieving process at that realization. Why? Because it challenges a concept long-ingrained in you, a myth: "My family has to be perfect. I have to be perfect. Oh, sure, we have flaws, but we're certainly not dysfunctional."

The realization about your dysfunctionality shatters one of your expectations. It shames you. It depresses you. And—hopefully—you go through the grieving process—all the way through it, no matter how long and hard it is. Because then you heal. You move on.

You see, taking the case of the family, when you finally come to an understanding of them, you can come to love them. This is what the Big Book of AA means when it says, *Love them, pray for them, let them be who they are.* When you go through the grieving process, you accept the fact that you cannot control your family—and never could. You accept who they were, who they are, and who you were and are. That understanding is the beginning of detachment with love.

And what of those people who really did hurt you? What if you are an incest survivor? A rape victim? How could you possibly come to love the perpetrator? Is that even possible? It is. Over time. The key is that, as you work on yourself, you understand more about all human beings, even those who have hurt you seriously. You will never like what they did to you. You may not particularly like them as people either. But understanding them is the beginning of acceptance, of accepting the fact that what they did is their issue now, not yours. And acceptance is the beginning of love. Think, for example, of the soldiers of our own generation, those who fought in Viet Nam—on both sides. It was a brutal war: napalm, booby traps, guerilla warfare. Yet today, in interviews, both sides reach out in reconciliation and respect. They'll never *like* what the other did during the war. Just as they may not like what *they* did during the war. But they came to understand it and accept it, which is a big step toward healing and love. What good would it do to hold each other hostage to the past?

TWELVE STEP TOOLS OF RECOVERY

In Twelve Step programs, we have what we formally call "tools of recovery." We have already covered these in some detail, so I'll simply review them here. They are, basically: meetings, the phone, journaling. We also include slogans, but we'll cover them separately, looking at the concepts behind some of the key slogans.

Regarding meetings, this refers to your attending group meetings with your Recovery Family. These are people you feel safe with in discussing your issues. These are people who will also teach you to listen and learn; you listen to their stories and issues, and learn that you are not the only one with problems. These people will not shame you, make you feel as though you there is something wrong with you for discussing your issues. On the flip side of this, did you ever try discussing your issues with people who are not in recovery? How did you feel afterwards? A little weird? Embarrassed? At the very least, you'll get a polite silence. At worst, you will activate your sense of shame, because your "audience" will not be interested in your problems.

At meetings, you share. Sharing is a way of processing. Processing is a way of releasing yourself from issues, of accepting your past, making peace with it, and moving on to your spiritual growth.

The phone is another tool. A woman I knew once called me because she was going through all sorts of turmoil and needed to talk it out. But I was out. My voice mail was on. She left a message for me to please, please, please call her so she could talk to someone she trusted. By the time I got home, there was a second message on the tape, telling me not to bother calling because, realizing I might not get home soon, she had called someone from a group she attended. They had talked things out. She was OK. I can't make it any simpler. The phone is a valuable tool of recovery. It is literally a line to people with whom you can share safely, people who will not activate your shame when you need to discuss personal things.

Journaling we already covered in some detail. Suffice it to repeat that it is a way of processing. Also, if you use the method prescribed before—keeping a negative and positive journal and eventually discarding the negative—you will watch your positive journal grow, even as the negative issues shrink in importance.

SLOGANS

I'll cover a few of the Twelve Step slogans here. Most were coined by the early AA movement, but, just as the Twelve Step method for AA has been adapted to so many other problems, like codependency, so have the slogans been adapted. You've probably seen most of them on bumper stickers. You might think they're corny. But slogans—any slogans—are powerful because they can charge people's emotions. In this case, they remind you to stick with the positive and stop beating yourself up, which is, of course, a key to shame reduction.

Easy Does It

Easy Does It is one of the most popular of the Twelve Step slogans. If it applies to AA, it applies at least fifteen times more to us codependents. Why? Because we have this disease: we want everything yesterday. People come into my lectures, which are advertised as a sixteen-week series. They see my tapes, buy them, take them home, and listen to them all in one night. They want the "cure." They want problems that have developed over a lifetime to go away overnight. It doesn't work that way. Recovery is a process. And the first slogan reminds us of that. *Easy Does It.* Slow down. Let it happen. Stop trying to CONTROL everything.

Inch By Inch

Inch By Inch is the second slogan. It reminds us that good, healthy progress probably works something like, *Five steps forward, two back.* In other words, don't shame yourself by thinking that progress is straight up. If you think that, when you slip—which most of us do—you'll beat yourself up and shame yourself, thinking that there's something wrong with you. Remember, as a codependent, you have been hurt. You do not trust. Healing and learning to trust take time. Which is why we say *Inch By Inch.*

One Day At A Time

One Day At A Time is the next slogan. It is one of the most beautiful ways of doing shame reduction work, and it is very special. One other thing: it is the only way possible to do shame reduction work—or anything else, for that matter. You can only live your life one day at a time. Probably all of us want to project into the future: *Where will I be in recovery seven months from now?* And we will compare ourselves to other people in recovery: *He seems to be doing so much better than me. What's wrong with me?* Nothing is wrong with you. You will work things out at your own pace, one day at a time. And this goes hand-in-hand with another slogan from AA: *Yesterday, Today, Tomorrow.* Yesterday is your teacher. Today is the day you try to apply the lessons you learned. Tomorrow isn't here yet. To put it another way from Eastern philosophy: Live beautifully in the present, and you'll automatically have a beautiful past and future.

Think, Think, Think

Think, Think, Think. Oh, did I have a problem with this one! As a codependent, I realized early on in recovery that one of my problems was *too much thinking!* Then I heard this slogan telling me to think more. But that's not the message. It's not telling me to think *more.* It's telling me to think *properly.*

Don't forget that many of us are compulsive people. As such, we often make snap decisions and then regret them; in other words, the decisions shame us. So to reduce shame, take the time to think things out. As an example, my wife has a little rule that drives the kids crazy but is good for us all. She tells them that if they're going to ask for something important, expect an answer in three days, no sooner. They get angry about it. But that's OK. What my wife is really doing is giving herself room to make important decisions properly. So, in the long run, everyone is happier about the answers they get.

So don't think you have to give answers to people right away—or that you have to respond to them at all, in some cases. That's a fetish that we codependents have. The reality is—the healthy way is—someone asks a question or expects something of you, you have the right to ask for information and take the time to process it, to think about it. Then you can respond as you see fit.

But for the Grace of God, There Go I

But for the Grace of God, There Go I. Even if you don't believe in God, you can see the sense in this. One of the things we have done to ourselves over years and years as codependents is be very hard on ourselves, very judgmental. Guess what? We applied the same patterns to others; we were very judgmental of them. But, as we get further along in recovery, this slogan reminds us how lucky we are. We are making progress. When we see someone who is not making progress, we don't criticize them. We empathize with them. Because we have been where they are.

Now, again, as when we talked about love, empathizing with someone doesn't necessarily mean that you'll like them. You see, the people who come into your life are your teachers. And some teachers are tough. You hate them. You might even want to kill them sometimes, it gets that extreme. But they are there for you to learn. And many philosophies say that you will keep meeting the same kind of people, the same kind of situations, until you learn the lesson you are supposed to learn from them. Let me give you an example.

A man in one of my groups was having a major problem with a co-worker, who was, in fact, a very negative, critical person. Being a good codependent, the man in my group had tried to please the other person so that person wouldn't be so critical and would actually become a friend. Eventually, after it finally sunk in, the man realized that this other person was almost pathologically negative; he wasn't going to change. Worse, when you treated him nice, he often repaid with bitterness, backbiting, and criticism. So the man started getting desperate to avoid the co-worker. Since that was almost impossible, he actually thought about quitting his job. When he ruled that out, he finally realized that he would have to establish some pretty definite boundaries in dealing with the co-worker. He would have to avoid certain conversations, not get into anything personal with the co-worker, and so on. The co-worker was just one of those people who seemed to take politeness for weakness; you just couldn't strike a happy chord with him.

That, I think, was the lesson the man had to learn: set boundaries. The co-worker was his teacher, even though at one point the man hated him for the misery he caused. But once the man did set boundaries, the more he got into recovery and applied the principles in that situation, the less the other person bothered him. In fact, the more the man worked on his own shame issues, the more he saw that the co-worker's problem had a lot to do with shame; the co-worker was, in fact, an Adult Child of an alcoholic father, though he could not admit it. The more the man understood the co-worker, the less power the co-worker had to upset him; the man was detaching from the situation, realizing that whatever issues were triggering the hostility between them were the co-worker's issues, not his. Eventually, he could empathize with the co-worker's plight. The co-worker had become his own shame, was stuck in the issue. The man could be grateful that he wasn't in the same boat any more.

In my own experience, I took the test for the seminary when I was in eighth grade. Two of us took it. I passed. The other guy didn't. I became a priest. I'm now writing this book. The other guy is serving a life sentence for murder. I often wonder what would have happened to me if he had passed the test and I flunked. So I can understand the wisdom in, *There But for the Grace of God...*

This might be a little hard to understand, but everything you do to someone else is a reflection of what you are doing to yourself on the inside. You judge yourself by the same scale you judge others. So learning the value of the slogan is actually giving yourself a break, because it teaches you to be less judgmental.

Let Go, Let God

Let Go, Let God. It's amazing how many of us, when we first hear this slogan, don't know what the "Let go" part refers to. Let go of what? Basically, let go of control. The fact is that you do not control much in this life anyway. Many philosophies say this in a basic way: concentrate on the process, let the results take care of themselves. You do not control the results. But, if you make a sincere effort at something, if you work on you and your part, the rest will take care of itself. That's the general idea behind the slogan, but it also has practical application for us codependents.

A friend of mine translated the slogan for me in the following way. Let Go: G-O—Garbage Out. Let God: G-O-D—Good Orderly Direction in. Let go of anything negative, anything that is sick, that eats away at me and destroys me. There is an old, old saying: We are only as sick as our secrets. Our secrets are the things we are ashamed to admit. If we follow the HOW of the recovery program—**H**onesty, **O**penness, **W**illingness—we will share our secrets with safe people, process them, and finally let them go.

We all have skeletons in our closet. Every so often those suckers rattle around. But if we finally face them we realize that they are just that: skeletons. They, like everything else in our lives, the positive and the negative, are our teachers. So let go of the hold they have on you and you reduce the shame in your life.

Also, let go of trying to control the process of recovery, of life. We try to force issues, face them all at once and get rid of them. It doesn't work that way. Let go of trying to force your recovery and let it happen in time. Concentrate on the process of your life, on trying to live a healthy life, and leave the results to your Higher Power, Whoever or Whatever that is.

THE BATTERY THEORY

To sum up on the tools of shame reduction, I like to refer to what I call the Battery Theory. You see, so many of us obsess with trying to get rid of the negative in our lives. We don't want any negative in our present, but that is impossible. People and events will bring negativity into your life. You cannot control that. Often it will happen unintentionally. People will shame you without even knowing it and vice versa. We also try to deny the negative in our past, and that, too, is impossible. In fact, it leads to denial and all sorts of other psychological pathology, and that leads us into the craziness of codependency, into depression, addiction, anxiety, and all the rest. And many of us try to avoid negativity in the future, which means they live in fear of negativity. Ever live in fear? It sucks.

The only logical thing to do is accept negativity as part of life. It's like a battery. A fully charged battery is half negative, half positive. It is the balance that gives the battery its power. If you doubt this, go out and disconnect either terminal from your car battery, the negative or the positive. Guess what? Your car won't start. You need both poles. You need balance.

You need the same balance in your life. If we are healthy, we are 50-50, balanced, positive and negative. Does this mean we walk around acting positively half the time and negatively the other half? No. It means that we accept our negative side, learn from it, and act in a healthy way. I once heard a company executive say in time of a business crisis: "Crunch time brings out the best or worst in a manager." Crunch time was the crisis, a negative situation for managers to deal with. Some buckled down and worked through it. Others panicked and started doing all kinds of negative stuff, like pointing fingers at others, blaming them for the problem. It's the same with us, with all human beings. If I have a negative issue, some trauma in my past, I can face it, learn from it, and move on, or I can point fingers and wallow in it.

I have been running all sorts of programs over the past thirty years. I have seen all sorts of people in half-way houses, prisons, and hospitals. Some of them have done horrendous things. But once they began treatment and were honest, open, and willing, they accepted the negative in their lives, learned from it, and grew past it. It is the person who shuts down and refuses to deal with shame issues who becomes sicker and sicker and gets caught in the spiral of drastic negative behavior.

I know of one woman, for example, who didn't—couldn't—honestly approach recovery until she was well on in life. Finally, in one of our sessions, she faced her major shame issue head-on. She had been sexually abused by her father—for *nine years!* She had never told anyone. She had denied it, kept it inside, and it had basically ruined her life up to that point. She had been unable to sustain a close relationship with anyone. Quite simply, she didn't trust anyone. How could she, when she couldn't even trust her own father? But when she finally opened up and started talking about the issue, all sorts of other shaming episodes came out as well. It was like cracking a dam, with all the water suddenly gushing out—things she had done and other things that had been done to her that she was ashamed of. That session was the beginning of her shame reduction process.

I know first-hand, as most codependents do, what shame can do to you. I did my first Twelve Step inventory in 1978. It was the first time I approached many of my issues. Up to that point, I had avoided the pain of facing those issues by burying myself in my food addiction. I used food to embalm me, to anaesthetize my feelings. Then, when I finally faced the issues and did the inventory, all that I could write about was the negative, the negative, the negative. It was almost as though nothing positive had ever occurred in my life. That was also difficult to experience. But as time went by, as I handled my food addiction and worked on shame reduction, the positive finally appeared. I now look at life in a much, much different light. I can appreciate life as a gift.

I cannot stress enough that the core issue for codependents is shame.

SERENITY

In closing on shame reduction, I remember something my father once told me that had a lot of wisdom in it. He said, "Vince, if you want to know if a man is a good carpenter, all you have to do is look at his tools." A good tradesman takes care of his tools, honors them. It's the same when we discuss shame reduction. We covered several tools you can use to do the work. They are not something that I created. They come from many sources. They work. But you have to use them, keep them sharp. Making decisions, setting boundaries, working with slogans, sharing with a Recovery Family—all takes work.

There is one other tool I would like to introduce you to. It has nothing to do with religion, though it is called a prayer, the Serenity Prayer. It is, in reality, a formula for living. It is very short. Yet it contains all the principles you need to recover from codependency.

The Serenity Prayer

God, grant me the Serenity
to accept the things I cannot change,
Courage to change the things I can,
And Wisdom to know the difference.

THE MOST POWERFUL SHAME REDUCTION TOOL

In my own experience, I have found the Serenity Prayer to be the most powerful of shame reductions tools. If you have a problem calling it a prayer, call it a formula. If you have a problem with the concept of a God outside of yourself, think of God as yourself fully developed. The important thing is to look at the concept behind the prayer. But before we get into that, let's look at some other things that shame does to us.

First, you have probably heard it said that many of us, especially codependents, give away our power. In terms of shame, this means that we think so little of ourselves that we look to other people for approbation, or confirmation. To put it in blunt terms, we need other people to like us. We can't stand it when they don't like us. We give them power over us because we give them power over our emotions. If they are nice to us, we are happy; if they are not nice, we are sad—or even clinically depressed and anxious. It is as simple as that. Other people rule our emotions. If we didn't suffer from toxic shame, we wouldn't care what other people thought of us. We would have a strong enough concept of self to rule our own emotions; we would be at peace just doing the best we could.

Second, shame also charges normal events in life so that they overwhelm us. For example, in my own experience, I suffered what used to be called a "nervous breakdown" in 1972. Ironically enough, my toxic shame contributed heavily to the breakdown, then made me feel even worse about it. I was mortified that I had the stigma of having been in a mental ward. But now, after a lot of shame reduction work, I see things much differently. I am actually grateful that I had the episode because it started me on the path to recovery. Now, instead of being paralyzed with shame about it, I see it as just another one of my teachers.

Third, shame basically intensifies our addictions—no matter what the addiction is: alcohol or other drugs, spending, sex, food...Shame makes us feel so bad that we run to our addictions to numb the pain, to embalm or anaesthetize ourselves. I believe that almost all relapse into addictions comes from being overwhelmed by our issues, particularly by shame.

In Twelve Step programs, we use the Serenity Prayer because it contains all the concepts we need to defuse the power of shame in our lives. I also point out that we are advised to repeat it over and over again. Why? Because shame has been programmed into us. Repetition of the prayer programs the healing concepts into our psyches as well. You might also experience a phenomenon with the prayer that people often report in other forms of therapy and work. They hear a concept, but they don't understand it right away. Maybe six months, or a year, or even more down the road of life, they hear it again and it sinks in. It's pretty much

the same with the Serenity Prayer. Its deeper meanings come
after you work with it for a while.

GOD GRANT ME

Whether you believe in God or not, you are probably familiar
with—have probably *experienced*—a very old adage: "Seek and
you shall find." That version of it comes from the Bible, but there
are other, more secular versions, like, "The harder you work, the
luckier you get." It's a beautiful concept. Look for something and
you will find it. Or, as some say, look for something, and *it* will
find *you*.

In the first three words of the prayer, we are looking for something: God. But remember how we define God in recovery. G-O-
D. GOOD ORDERLY DIRECTION. When you get a sense of order, of
direction, in your life, you become calm and open—open to learn
from situations, rather than be overwhelmed by them. And we
said that shame tends to overwhelm us. So we are asking not to
be overwhelmed by anything, especially shame.

THE SERENITY TO ACCEPT
THE THINGS I CANNOT CHANGE

This is simple to grasp but usually difficult to live by. It is a
fact of life that you cannot change people, cannot "fix" anyone,
cannot "rescue" anyone, cannot save anyone. You are, in fact,
powerless over most things in life, if not everything. Thank God!
Once I get the concept, I can stop trying to control events and
people. That's a problem with us codependents: we are control
freaks. We think if we don't control everything, some catastrophe
will happen. Yet the illusion of our controlling things is just that:
an illusion. When you finally get that, you can also get the point
that you can lower your expectations of people and things. And
when you do that you lower your own sense of shame. For example, if I do not expect everyone to like me automatically, then
when I run across someone who doesn't like me, I just accept it,
rather than beat myself up wondering why I'm not likeable.

Acceptance is 95% of recovery. Accept your parents for who they are. Accept other people for who they are. Accept circumstances for what they are. Stop trying to organize them, control them, fix them to be the way *you think* they should be. Does this mean that you have to accept misery? No. Remember, we said before, one of the peculiarities of recovery, as testified to by so many people who have been through it, is that if you work on yourself everything else seems to take care of itself.

There's an old analogy comparing life to a butterfly. If you try to capture it, control its beauty, you just kill it. You have to let it flow, be free. For example, to refer back to the concept of the Big Book of AA, maybe there are people you have been trying to control, trying to get to see things your way. Forget it. You cannot control them. So just love them, pray for them, and let them be who they are. Use your energy to work on you. To take the example further, so many of us have problems with our parents. We want them to accept us—on our terms. So we play games with them when they don't. We try to explain to them what they're doing wrong, get them to change. But doing that implies that there is something wrong with them. It shames them. In turn, they tell us what we are doing wrong, and so we are shamed by implication as well. Remember we called it the Shame Game. But it takes two to play a game. So if you stop, just accept them for who they are and realize that they'll never give you what you want on your terms, the game ends. The shame is diminished, or, as we say in the process of recovery, it is reduced.

I think of a client whose father wanted him to take over the family business. The client didn't want to; to him it was boring. He gave up the business and went into his own profession—but only after wrangling with the father, trying to convince him that he was doing the right thing. My client finally realized that he would never convince his father, never get his approval for going into his own profession. It was understandable, from the father's viewpoint; he had built the business through the Great Depression and it had kept his family fed. To him, keeping the business was like a matter of life and death; lose it and you don't eat in tough times. That was the father's experience. But the son finally went into his own profession and stopped trying to get his father's approval. When the father raised the subject, he'd listen for a while and then change the subject. It saved a lot of grief.

There's a saying in Twelve Step programs that people get into recovery when they finally get *sick and tired of being sick and tired!* So, in the first part of the prayer, we are asking for the direction to find acceptance of reality, of what *is*. We are asking to detach from things over which we have no control. Hopefully, in time, that detachment will be with love, not anger. For example, the client mentioned above can still love his father, even though they can't agree on something important to both. If you can detach, especially with love, you will have serenity. Remember, you will probably not detach with love, but with anger, at first. The love comes later, as you grow spiritually. Serenity is not a zombie-like state. It is the foundation for happiness. Depression, anxiety, addictions, and all the other craziness of codependency cannot exist where there is serenity.

COURAGE TO CHANGE THE THINGS I CAN

Don't confuse courage with insanity. The guy on the motorcycle charging down the expressway way above the speed limit isn't courageous. He's insane. People who finally decide to deal with the tough issues in their lives are courageous. Being open to change and grow is courageous. In fact, if you did a psychological study on the guy on the cycle, you'd probably find that he was acting insane because he wasn't dealing with his issues. He's showing false courage as a way to avoid his real issues. It's a shame. You've probably heard the saying that the real heroes are the quiet heroes. They are the ones with inner strength.

Now, if you get the courage to face your issues, to grow and change, what is it that you change? Well, the only thing in the world you can really change is you. Zip. Period. Amen. And, to say it again, that's a relief! Once you understand that concept, you can stop worrying about trying to change anybody else. You are free to concentrate on working on yourself.

But working on what? *On being open to looking at yourself,* looking at what has become your normal, your patterns. Are they really healthy for you? Or are they sick? If they are sick, do you have *the willingness to change and grow*? If you do, you will start learning about yourself. This is the beginning of the process of *developing a relationship with yourself.* It takes courage, because you have to embrace everything about yourself, including your limitations and handicaps. You also have to acknowledge your sick patterns and have the courage to change them, let them go, and replace them with new experiences and ways of acting. For example, many of us are constantly battling other people in our lives, like parents or spouses or children or friends. We are hurting them, shaming them, and doing the same to ourselves. But guess what? Painful as it is, we don't want to let go, don't want to change, because that battling has become our normal. We do it automatically. Changing will take effort, will be painful in itself, at least until we get used to new patterns in our lives.

I can draw some analogies to how this works. For example, none of us want to be in a hospital for any length of time. But guess what? People who experience long hospital stays experience anxiety when they are finally discharged. As unpleasant as the hospital stay was, it became their normal, their routine. Getting back into normal life is frightening, painful. The same with a stay in prison. Believe it or not, long-term prisoners experience similar anxiety, and for the same reasons, when they are released. They want to change, want the freedom, but it is also anxiety-producing to give up the "normal" of prison life.

So courage is having the willingness to change. This is such an important topic for us codependents that I will devote the last chapter to covering it in detail. As codependents, we become so wrapped up in our issues, so wrapped up in trying to change *others*, that we have a very difficult time letting things go. It's as though we have to stay in there, battling to change people and things we can't change, so that *we* never change. Yet change is closure. It is healing. It is moving on. Remember the analogy of the phoenix rising from the ashes. From change, from an ending, rises a new beginning.

I'd like to share an example from my own experience. When my wife and I got married, she had children from another marriage. They went through some pretty rough changes coming to grips with the fact of our marriage. When they did, I wanted them to understand, to be cooperative, and to accept the marriage—and I wanted it as soon as possible. That's codependency; I wanted to control their emotions. Now, however, I saw another couple go through the same thing, and I can look at it objectively. Children in such a situation would have to be abnormal *not* to have a reaction. After all, their whole life, their whole world, is changing drastically. They have to go through some changes with it. And it takes time—and courage. If they are equipped and taught how to face the change, accept it instead of denying what is happening, they get past the mourning of the old ways, past the anger and denial, and come to peace with it. If not, it becomes a major issue for them. Just as wanting to control my step-children's reactions was becoming an issue for me.

COURAGE IN RECOVERY

People in recovery are some of the most courageous people I've ever met. First, let's repeat something. I'm not just talking about recovery from drugs or alcohol. I'm talking about recovery from any form of codependency. Recovery from depression, from anxiety, from food addictions, sexual addictions, spending addictions...Recovery from anything creating insanity in our lives. Why does it take courage? Let's look at a few scenarios.

For example, people who decide to put down the drink...That probably means that the whole direction of their lives, everything they know as normal, will change. To get to that point, they already went through a grieving process. They stopped denying that alcohol was a problem. They stopped bargaining that they could still drink occasionally, have the proverbial—and mythical—one or two. They went through the anger and depression coming to grips with their addiction, and finally came to accept it. What then? They could no longer rely on alcohol to embalm themselves in times of stress; they had to feel their feelings. They had to give up their barroom friends. They probably had to face the fact that they were lacking true intimacy in their other relationships, because they were avoiding that with alcohol, and work on developing that. All strange. All new. Sometimes painful. And it takes courage.

A client I had once complained to me that he had stopped drinking, stopped drugs, and his life was in turmoil. I said, "Congratulations, you're on the right path." He had to find the courage to stay on the path, stay in recovery, even when he slipped once in a while.

If you stick with recovery, however, you will discover something: THE GREATEST HEALING SPOT IN THE WHOLE WORLD IS INSIDE OF YOU, NOT ON THE OUTSIDE. That means that you are going to start to *feel* differently, feel a power you never had, or only had so long ago that you virtually forgot it. You will probably realize that much of this strength comes from reducing your feelings of shame; the negative is going out, the positive coming in. You will experience and be conscious of your own personality changing. And you will see how courage builds on itself; ever hear the successful sports teams talking about how winning is contagious? It's the same principle. I call people in true recovery walking miracles, because I see them developing the courage to change and grow, to be open, to listen, to take Good Orderly Direction. I see the contagious positive effects this has on them.

So "Courage to change the things I can..." means the courage to change *YOURSELF*.

AND WISDOM TO KNOW THE DIFFERENCE

Wisdom is a gift. It only comes from experience, from openness, from learning, from hard knocks, from scars, and from all the growth we go through in the course of our lives. Wisdom is the art and gift of *being able to set boundaries*. I can give you two quick examples, one light, the other a little heavier.

The first is a joke I like to play. I'm well into my fifties and I play basketball. So many times I get these kids—twenty-somethings—coming up to me and challenging me to play a game of One-on-One. I say, "OK. Let's put two bucks on it. But here's the rules. We play One-on-One-By One. Which means the winner has to have a hundred points to win. The wisdom I'm practicing here is that most twenty-year-olds don't have the patience for this game. See, you're probably talking about four hours or so to get the hundred points. Most of them, in fact, get bored and don't even finish the game. My wisdom tells me that I'll never beat them in a run-and-shoot, but that they don't have the patience, the endurance, to play my game.

The second example is like one I've already given you. My wife and I were invited to a barbecue. When we got there, the first thing we noticed were about four kegs of beer on tap. The crowd was already half-tanked. Knowing how it would go from there, I also knew that this wasn't my or my wife's idea of fun. The old me would have felt obligated to stay. I would have gotten more miserable and critical as the night went on, and would have basically wasted a night having a rotten time. But now I know I can set boundaries. So my wife and I just went around and paid our respects, then made the rounds again saying good-bye. No big deal. People have a right to get drunk. I don't have the right to judge them. But I do have the right to do what suits me. As it turned out, my wife and I went to dinner and had a great time, a quiet, peaceful time. And the people at the party had their own good time.

The wisdom of recovery gives you balance. Balance is not criticizing other people for what they do. Sometimes we tend to get so self-righteous: "I don't drink. So the rest of the world shouldn't drink either!" That's not balance. Balance is working on yourself and letting other people be where they need to be. And the beauty of the program can be summed up in that very brief phrase: Work on *YOU* and everything else will take care of itself.

Wisdom is also knowing that we each have to work at our own pace, at our own program. Sometimes we look at other people and figure we have to be where they are, have to work the program they're working. Our own progress isn't good enough, we think. I still do this myself. And yet I believe our Higher Power guides us back to where we should be—if we are open to the direction. For example, I work out at a gym. I have a program designed for me personally, for a fifty-something-year-old man of my size and weight. But, one time, I saw a young guy doing some pretty strenuous exercises, and I got the notion that I should be pushing myself harder, doing what he was doing. So I did. And pulled a tendon. I had to wait for it to heal before getting back to my own program again. That taught me something. And it reminded me that the same wisdom applies in recovery.

A wise yogi once told his students to take things slowly. Make the effort and leave the results to a Higher Power. Don't push too fast. He used the example of some of the youth in the late Sixties. They wanted enlightenment—and they wanted it *NOW!* So rather than go through the effort of meditation and prayer and yoga or whatever, they "dropped acid," took LSD. And some of them did get a taste of enlightenment all at once. One of his own students, in fact, claimed to have seen God. But guess what? None of them wanted to repeat the experience. Whatever they saw, or thought they saw and experienced, they weren't ready for it. It scared the hell out of them. Wisdom is learning to work your own program at your own pace, knowing what you can do and cannot do.

PRACTICING THE PRAYER

Do we always do what the prayer says? Of course not. We slip sometimes. We forget. That's part of life and recovery, too. You slip. You get hurt. You learn from the pain. You go back and do what you need to do. Set your boundaries and work within them. When you don't, you wind up reactivating your shame and the shame in other people.

Another way of putting it is work within your limitations. Limitations are natural boundaries. Not only are they are normal part of life, they also free you from trying to do too much. For example, look at the prayer in relation to your own Family of Origin, whatever that is. Maybe you are in recovery and part of you—that Child Within—desperately wants them to be in recovery, too. That's a very normal feeling for us to have. The child in us wants to make everything better. But wisdom, the adult in us, reminds us that we cannot control anyone else. We cannot make them be where we want them to be. So we set our boundaries with our family accordingly. We do what is healthy for us. We do not shame them in the process. So certain things, for example, you'll be able to talk about with them, share with them. But some things you will not be able to share with them. It might make things a little superficial between you sometimes, but that is OK.

Some time ago our treatment center was having a problem with our landlord. Some things in the building were broken and long overdue to be fixed. In fact, we had contacted him many times only to have him ignore us. Part of me—the little kid inside—wanted to throw a tantrum. Grab a hammer or something and go pound some sense into the landlord. The adult in me said something else. First, just repeating our complaints to the guy wasn't going to work. But there was something between that and the "hammer solution" that I could try. So I invited him out to lunch. It gave me a chance to explain that we were a treatment center and how the building problems were affecting services to our clients. I explained it calmly and gently. And guess what? I learned something. All along, he had never realized what we did in our offices. He thought they were just business offices, nothing to do with traffic from clients, like the rest of the offices in the building. Once he understood what we did, he realized that the needed repairs were a higher priority for us. And he sent a crew to fix things.

Maybe it was a coincidence. But my wisdom tells me that if I had strapped on my armor, so to speak, and gone to do battle with him, he would have had no choice but to strap on his armor to defend himself. It would have become a grudge match.

So one thing the Serenity Prayer has taught me, and that I try to practice, is that you solve problems through healing and gentleness. Living the Prayer also means knowing that I need direction. Not just sometimes. Not just until I'm "cured" of my codependency; wisdom tells me that recovery is not only a process, but a *life-long* process. I need direction in my life. And I need courage to follow that direction. I need the wisdom to know that I can only work on me and that I need to work on me till ten days or so after I'm dead and I need courage to do that work. The

Prayer has also taught me that if I run into something I need to do but can't do myself, I get help. You keep it that simple. That's what living the Serenity Prayer is all about.

There is another aspect of the Prayer, of wisdom, that we experience as we work on ourselves. I call it "Letting Go of Taboos." It's not easy for codependents to do that. It causes a lot of pain, anxiety. The taboos come from the most powerful rules ever laid on us: childhood rules. They are deep, deep in our psyche. As I cover them in the next chapter, I think you will see the wisdom in the Serenity Prayer when it asks for the *courage* to change the things we can. Letting go of taboos is painful. Facing that pain, getting through it, takes courage.

I also have another name for this process of Letting Go of Taboos. I call it "God As I Understand Him."

God as I Understand Him

THE TABOOS

The Taboos in our lives are part of the shame process. They are part of the Original Shame messages given to us in the very early stages of our lives, so they become part of our deepest fiber. They are presented to us as something sacred. They are never to be challenged. And when you come to the point in your life that you do challenge them, as you inevitably must, they cause you a great deal of pain, usually in the form of depression and anxiety fueled by Guilt and Shame and Fear. The taboos are given to us by the Family Systems that we talked about in Chapter II: Family of Origin, Society, Religion, Peer Groups, and the Media, or our secular culture. The taboos are basically presented to you as absolute truth, with the warning that if you ever challenge them something will get you, something bad will happen to you.

As an example, when I was a kid I was taught that you never question God. If you do, He will punish you. So I spent most of my life being afraid of God. After all, I was human. I was making my share of mistakes and questioning things about God and life, so I kept looking over my shoulder, wondering when He was going to get me. Even the term "He" in referring to God was a stumbling block. Today I realize that God, *as I understand Him,* works out of reality, and, as such, can be a He, She, or even something beyond those labels—anything that helps us better understand the Higher Power.

Taboos are absolutes. If you live your life around absolutes, you are putting yourself in a position of judging. Shame naturally flows from judging, because when you find someone who doesn't agree with your absolutes, you try to invalidate their point of view, try to make them feel that there is something fundamentally wrong with them. By the way, that's called Control. Also, if you have to try to convince everybody that you are right, it means that you yourself are not convinced—otherwise, you would simply stand back and let people find the truth for themselves; you wouldn't feel a need to force it on them.

TABOOS KEEP YOU FROM YOUR HIGHER POWER

I call my personal Higher Power "God." As we said before, you can identify your Higher Power *as you understand* your Higher Power. But generally you come to understand your Higher Power through the workings of yourself and your environment, including the people and things you experience. Since the entire world, including you, is constantly changing, you can see where absolute rules, the Taboos, can keep you from understanding your Higher Power. Basically, absolutes and change don't go well together. If your whole experience is telling you one thing, and your taboos insist on something else, and you insist on clinging to your taboos, you will experience shame. It's a simple concept: Either the taboos are wrong, or you are wrong; if you insist on honoring the taboos, you invalidate yourself, make you think there is something wrong with you, which is shame.

What makes the taboos so strong is that they are usually given to us as Original Shame Messages. They are sunk into the earliest parts of our life, the roots of our psyche. Let's look at some of the common ones.

Most of us are taught that God is a God of fear, of guilt, of trepidation and punishment. If you believe in that concept, you begin to look at the world as something to be feared, as something bad. And you begin to experience yourself that way; after all, you are part of this world. What greater shame experience can you have than to think of yourself as something bad?

Why was God described to us that way? Control. Religion wanted to control us. Society wanted to control us. So God was used as a God of guilt to control us. "If you do something wrong, go against the rules, you will be punished." For those of us who accepted that, we constantly looked over our shoulders to see if we were doing the right thing or if someone was coming to punish us. That, by the way, is a form of anxiety. In my own case, I was constantly scared and very hard on myself.

What I realize today is that this concept of the Higher Power is a taboo, something used to control people through fear. It is unhealthy. Today, I realize that I am allowed to have a God of my own understanding. A God of my belief process. A God that works for me. I am allowed to develop in my life whatever is healthy for me. That is part of what the Higher Power is to me, as I understand Him. He is a God of health.

I still have twinges of guilt, though. Every once in a while the fact that I challenge the old taboo, the old concept of God, brings those twinges. It is something we must work on as we grow.

I'll give you another example, what I call an outrageous example. When I was growing up, in the 40's, one of the taboos that many people honored was "Never fly in a plane." Many of the people in my neighborhood, including my own mother, shared that fear. It was passed on to me. So that, even today, when I'm walking to board a plane, I almost expect my mother to pop up and start scolding me—and mom has been dead for well over a decade.

Think of your own taboos. Think of your personal outrageous taboos, as well as those passed on to us by society and religion and peer groups. For example, what did we learn about Country? Remember the saying, "My country right or wrong..." My country can never be wrong. Yet we know now that countries are made up of people, and people are fallible, and so countries are fallible.

Or think of a Church, organized religion. We are also taught that our religion cannot be wrong. Whatever it teaches us is infallible. Yet, when I was a clergyman I was asked to teach a course in African-American history. This was back in the early 70's, and a course like that was rare, something new. I got the job because I was stationed in an African-American parish at the time. But what did I know about African-American history? So I just followed the book. And *I* learned something. It blew me away. I learned that the slaves on plantations were taught catechism—religion—but it was different from what the slave owners' children were taught. In both catechisms it posed the question, "Who made you?", and it gave the answer, "God." It then asked, "Who are you supposed to obey?" In the owners' catechism the answer was God. In the slaves, it was God *and the master*. So the slaves were given a taboo, a sacred, an absolute. They were programmed to believe that the slave owner was equal to God.

ONE ULTIMATE AUTHORITY

Today, I have come to understand that there is only one legitimate ultimate authority: your Higher Power *as you understand your Higher Power.* You come to understand your Higher Power by being open to learning, to growth, which means that sometimes you have to be open to discarding the taboos in your life. Let's look at a few more examples to illustrate.

Just like the slave catechism, we codependents set people and things on an improper level. Basically, we set them above us, on pedestals. What we are doing is giving our power to them. What we want in exchange is to avoid the pain of growth. We put people on pedestals, make gods of them, and basically want them to tell us what to do, how to live. When you do that, you are doing a grave disservice to them and to yourself, because ultimately no one can live up to that god-like expectation. The people you put on pedestals will ultimately fall off the pedestal, will let you down. Then what? You are worse off than when you started. You see this often in relationships. We want someone who can tell us how to live, give us the answers. What you learn in recovery is that no one can do this for you. You must find your own answers. And sometimes you will not learn the answers to everything. That's OK. You'll find the answers you need to know. The rest you might struggle with and eventually let go, let be. It's a simple philosophy. You don't have to analyze everything to death.

What makes that simple philosophy difficult to live is that we are conditioned to feel that we can't possibly run our own lives, find our own answers. First, we are used to being given the "rules." Second, we feel so personally insignificant that we cannot possibly accept that we have the power to run our own lives. But we do. We are each unique, special. We each count. We each have the power to manage our own lives and make our own decisions.

Of course, we don't just give our power away to *people*. We also look to institutions to run our lives for us. One of these institutions is recovery itself; some people get into it and create the taboo that it has to be one way and one way only or it won't work. They never see that their own rigidity in approaching recovery is creating insanity for them. It's almost as though, instead of having the goal of joy and freedom from unhealthy things, their goal is following the rules, no matter what feelings that brings them.

The point is that things change. Even your sacreds change— whether or not you want them to. Even recovery changes for each of us. We must be open to grow and discover new things and put aside the old taboos.

THREE PRINCIPLES

I would like to share three basic principles that I learned in my own recovery. The first one we already touched on: Nothing is absolute. Life is change, is a process. Being open to change is healthy. Second, there are no sacreds. If you put a person, place, or thing on a pedestal, if you expect that person, place, or thing to run your own life, you are doing yourself and that person, place, or thing a disservice. An example for me is that when I was growing up I was taught that you only went to one Church, one denomination. If you violated that, something would happen to you. I still to this day don't know what was supposed to happen to me, but it was something vague and bad. Today, I realize that I can learn from any Church, from any source, if I am open to learn from it. For example, a Buddhist, so foreign to my own culture and upbringing, can teach me something if I am open to the teaching.

Also, in regard to being open in recovery, even people who are not in recovery can teach me. They can be your teachers. They might not be pleasant to be around. You might not like them or what they do. It might be painful. But you can learn from them if you are open. You can see this in process in a codependency meeting. So many times people will discuss how certain people or situations resurrect their codependency issues, for example, how they try to please people or institutions, even when this is unhealthy for them personally, or how they try to control other people or situations to get the approbation they so desperately need, or think they need. These are just some of the common codependency issues, of course. What you hear in a meeting is how people become open to learn about their issues by being open to the lessons that people and situations can teach them.

We are taught, and I think it is true, that all of us are created in the likeness of a Higher Power. *All* of us. No matter who the person is. Even the people behind bars. Which leads me to the third principle: God As I Understand Him. It's sort of an open-ended principle, because what it means is that I learn about my Higher Power by watching the unfolding of the people around me. Or, to put it another way, if we work on ourselves, discover who we are, build a relationship with ourselves, discover the gift of ourselves as unique people and participate in the process of life, then we discover a God as we understand a God through us, through our own experience. It might not be an easy concept to grasp. That's OK. It's not as simple, say, as telling you that, Oh,

Yeah, you see God is an old guy with a white beard who lives in the clouds and punishes us for some things and rewards us for others and only wants to be worshiped by one name and in one way and all the rest are wrong, and so on...Because the fact is that God as I understand Him is how He unfolds in my own life, how I came to be open and then saw my life change from depression and anxiety and addiction and care-taking and fantasizing and isolating and all sorts of other unhealthy behaviors to a healthy, fulfilling experience. And God as I understand Him also comes from having watched the same thing happen to other people, through their own individual paths, as well. That's why I call people in recovery walking miracles. It's like a miracle to see the change in people from the misery of codependency to the serenity of recovery.

THEOLOGY OF THE GUT

In my lectures, I like to share as many examples of the principles as I can to help my listeners understand them. By the examples, which I take from my own experience, you can also see that I didn't get the principles on the first pass either. I had to experience a lot of change, a lot of pain, a lot of growth before they started to sink in. I don't mean "sink in" to the brain; most of us can understand things on an intellectual level. I mean sink into the gut, into our feelings. If you look at depression and anxiety and the other manifestations of codependency as the terrible, hopeless feelings they are, you can understand that if the principles sink into the gut, if they cause my feelings to change for the better, they bring their own peace and serenity—which sure beats depression and anxiety. I call this the "Theology of the Gut." Like any theology, it takes practice.

One of my first experiences with this theology, with the principles, was in the seminary. I had a teacher, a priest who was ninety years old. I remember having this attitude, "What can this old guy teach me?" After all, I was going to be part of the new generation of priests, not as stodgy and stiff as the old generation. Maybe he picked this up, because one day in class he posed to me, "Vince, describe God." I didn't flinch. After all, I was twen-

ty-one, I knew everything. So I spouted off a textbook answer—
in fact, I gave him about fifteen descriptions from the books—
and was proud of my erudition. And he *laughed at me.* He said,
"You aren't hearing what I'm asking you." It only took a second
to get over my hurt; see, I quickly figured, "Oh, I forgot, he's in
his nineties. He can't handle the new definitions of God. He
wants the old ones." So I rattled off the old-fashioned definitions.

Now, let me pause here and look at the process of what was
going on. Maybe you'll see something familiar. In this exchange
with the old priest, I was giving him all kinds of power. I forgot
all about me, about the question, about learning. Basically what
I was trying to do was please him so he would give me a good
mark, maybe like me, praise me as a good student.

Fortunately, the old man, my teacher, wasn't caught up in my
game, my codependency. He simply tried the question a different
way: "Vince, what do you like to do the most?" That was easy. At
the time, I liked sitting after classes and studies and eating
pizza. I told him that. And he said, "Vince, God for you at this
moment in your life is eating pizza for eternity."

It wasn't exactly a textbook definition. But oddly I could
relate to it. And I can understand it much better today. What he
was saying was get in touch with your own life and realize that
God is connected deeply inside of you, and that as you begin to
experience a sense of yourself as a person you will begin to experience a God as you understand God and begin to develop a belief
process that works for you. And what works for you this week
might not work for you next week. You can learn something else
from another direction that will change your understanding of
yourself. Slowly, you develop a relationship with yourself, and so
you also develop a relationship with God, with a Higher Power,
because God created you. To state it yet another way, so many
times we go outside looking for the inside.

You can see God unfold in other ways around you, too. Let's
return, for example, to the concept of country. So many of us see
country as a sacred. Somewhere along the line we come to accept
that my country is never wrong; that you don't criticize country;
and, if you do criticize it, then you should leave it. There was that

old slogan in the 60's: AMERICA—LOVE IT OR LEAVE IT. Yet today we understand that we as a nation make mistakes. We can criticize ourselves. What's more, we feel that if we can't take our own criticism, we're not much of a country. We keep an open mind and learn as we go along. Our loyalty doesn't have to be so rigid. In fact, being open to criticism and growth is the beauty of our country, what makes us special among nations. It is healthy and as such is like watching God unfold in our experience of country.

In relationships, in family, when we remove the sacreds, we experience growth, and so come to know ourselves better and our Higher Power, as we understand that power, better. For example, whether or not we realized it—or realize it yet—we held it sacred to give our families all of our power, total loyalty. That translated into certain rules that we never broke. One was that the family could never show its dysfunction—not even to one another—not even when that dysfunction was driving everyone crazy. Everything had to be OK. There wasn't supposed to be any conflict, any struggle, any disagreement—at least, *meaningful* disagreement. Now we know better. We know that we are all dysfunctional, the world is dysfunctional, and so relationships are dysfunctional. And since family relationships are among the most powerful, their dysfunctionality is powerful. We can go around denying it or trying to make everything perfect, but I think we know where that leads. Or I can adjust. I can learn and unlearn things from my family and from any relationship.

I know a man whose father is eighty-one and has been an alcoholic for probably better than sixty of those years. And the man keeps trying to "fix" his father. He's been trying for the fourteen years that I've known him. He is obsessed with changing his father before his father dies. He feels that it's his duty. As a result he beats himself and his father half to death. He has no life of his own. He's blaming himself for his father's dysfunction, and his father doesn't have the slightest idea what he's talking about. The father just shakes his head when he sees him and says here comes my crazy son again, here he comes preaching. He even told the son that he should find a church and become a preacher. Basically the father also told him that yes, he's embalmed himself with alcohol but that's the way he wants to be, he's too old to change, and anyway this way they won't have to embalm him after he's gone. At least the father has a sense of humor.

But the son can't accept that, can't let go. As a result, he's put his father—or, more accurately, his father's alcoholism—on a pedestal. He's made a god out of it. He's given his life to it. After all, his life revolves around it. He has basically said it's his job to fix his father and if he doesn't, there's something wrong with him as a son. Recognize the issue? Shame. If the father doesn't change, there's something wrong with the son. We said that shame is hard to get over. It is no easy thing for the man to find the serenity in letting go of what he cannot change, in grieving his situation and letting it go, accepting it, and then moving on with his own life. If he did, he might even come to laugh at the situation. As a good codependent I never understood that; you can get to the point where you laugh at things, even when they're not funny. You can process shame and learn from it and grow from it.

In learning the Theology of the Gut you start to see, FEEL things. You look at expectations, yours and others'. You look at the status quo, traditions, things that have become our normals. Alcoholics in recovery have experienced it. They used to go down to the bar to see their friends, they hung out, they got drunk. It was normal. It was called fun. Now they see it as insane. Part of the reason they did it was in honor of the sacreds; if they didn't do it, their friends wouldn't like them, they'd be isolated. As good codependents, they had that desperate need for approval, for acceptance, to fit in. In recovery, they finally get the feeling in their gut: they don't need to look outside for approval. They can do what's healthy for them and experience serenity. They also know that they don't have to go around preaching to the guys who still go down to the bar and get drunk. They have no control over them. Everybody works on their own life, in their own way. And somehow serenity flows from that, from doing what you can, making your best effort.

In the Theology of the Gut you learn from your old pain and you experience new pain, but you don't stop there. For example, take someone, like me, who was overweight a good portion of their life. The old pain was the misery of the addiction, of embalming myself with food then feeling shamed and guilty and depressed and anxious about it—and then doing it again. The new pain is the pain of grieving, of realizing what I had been doing, of what it had cost me in life, how my life could have been without the addiction. But you work through that, realize that, first, there's nothing I can do about it now, and, second, that it was a teacher when I became open to learn from it, and that there was life after the addiction.

THE EXPERIENCE OF SIMPLICITY

In my lecture series, I like to sum up the message of this chapter with a few basic points, all of which are centered around simplicity. Because, when you think about it, as complicated and strange and different as some of the things we covered sound, they really boil down to a simple process. We feel pain in our lives, the pain of shame and guilt and fear and anger and whatever else. If we open ourselves to learning from the pain, we realize that we have to let go of things, have to take certain people, places, and things down off their pedestals, have to replace some old sacreds with a new, open way of living. We basically realize that what we learned and lived by maybe weren't healthy for us. We realize that we can't change what we were taught or experienced or did or didn't do. We pray for the courage to change our behavior to something healthy; we deal in the present. When we do that—*as* we do it—we experience something new, something very positive, something that brings a real joy to living.

I personally have lived this experience. Now, as good codependents—especially those of you going through depression and anxiety as you read this—you're thinking, "Yeah, Vince, that was you. You're different. But you don't know me. I just don't have it in me, don't feel it in me." Whatever. Let me share two FACTS with you.

In preface to the two facts, let me repeat that I told you up front that much of my philosophy of recovery is taken directly from Twelve Step programs. Well, the first Twelve Step meeting was an AA meeting. It occurred in the 30's. It consisted of two people—both of whom had been declared incurable—hopeless—alcoholics by the medical profession *and* themselves. Now here are the two facts.

First, as of 1993, there were *96,000* AA groups worldwide. Now add to that all the other groups that use the Twelve Step method: codependents, incest survivors, gamblers anonymous, overeaters anonymous, debtors anonymous, and so on. How many *millions* of people are experiencing their recovery through these programs?

Second, Step Twelve begins, "Having had a spiritual awakening..." Having *had*...Not *if.* That is what is formally called the Promise of the Program: you *will have* a spiritual awakening. If you *practice* the principles. And, if you read the Twelve Steps for any of the programs, you will see that they specifically address, by name, depression and anxiety and addiction and all the things you are experiencing that is making life seem hopeless. Having a spiritual awakening means getting beyond the suffering, getting into life, finally getting the Theology of the Gut.

Those are the two facts. I am not saying that the Twelve Steps is the only way to recovery. Let's not set up another sacred. I am only saying that I have experienced and witnessed the method work—and apparently so have millions of other people just like us. And let's face it...No matter how unique we think our problems are, no matter how much our codependency convinces us that we are hopeless, somewhere in those millions is someone who was just like us. Same problems.

It's a simple program. Watching it work shows me God as I understand Him. And it begins with a simple principle, which I will use to close this book. But, first, just let's remind ourselves that simple doesn't mean without effort.

Willingness
to Change and Grow

THE SIMPLEST PRINCIPLE

I have laid out many principles, many formulas, in this book. Some you have understood more than others. Some you might not understand at all. If you're like the rest of us looking for an end to codependency, an end to depression and anxiety, and the beginning of a fulfilling life, you might seem overwhelmed. You might be asking, fretting, "What will I do when I finish these last few pages? How can I actually begin to change my life?" My response is this: start by trying to be willing to change and grow. That's all. Just try to be willing.

That's it. Zip. Period. To begin your recovery or take it to the next level, just *try* to be willing to change and grow. And trust the process from there. The process works.

I said at the close of the last chapter that it's a simple principle. I also said that simple doesn't mean easy. Again, if you're like the rest of us, you will resist change, and you might not even be aware that you are resisting. So by trying, you develop a willingness to change and grow. That's how you start.

Don't forget, when you start to change you are going to challenge things that you have accepted as your normals. They might be things that cause you a lot of pain, but they are your normals; they are "comfortable," in a perverse way. When you move away from them, you move into unfamiliar ground, and, though that might be healthier and happier for you, it's going to be scary at first. That's why we resist change.

I share a story in my lectures. It goes back to when I was a priest. I was taking some college courses and we had exchange professors from Europe. One was a Jesuit from Belgium. He walked into class the first day, and there we were, all seminarians and priests and nuns with our desks so neat, our pens poised to take notes, like, "Give me the information so I can write it down." He walked up to the podium and said, "Hello." We answered in kind. Then he said, "What do you want to learn today?"

Nobody said anything. So he repeated the question. Nobody moved. So he said, "OK, let's go to lunch."

We went berserk. It was like, hey, we paid money for this, you're supposed to know what to teach! You're not teaching us anything! He said, "But I asked what you wanted to learn and you didn't say anything." We were really mad then. You see, as I understand now, we had been conditioned. The teacher teaches. We write it down and parrot it back. We get a good mark. Instead, after a while, he did lead us off to lunch. After we ate, he looked around the cafeteria and said, "Nice place. Nice lunch. And that's what we learned today, how to have a nice lunch."

In the later classes with that professor, we started to see what he was doing. He was challenging us, making us look inside and see what we needed to learn. He was giving us back our power. And we were petrified of that. We did not trust ourselves to ask for what we needed. We wanted to be told what we needed—by someone on a pedestal.

The point is that, when something new comes along, it shakes you up. Even when that something new is good, something positive, it can shake you up. As noted earlier, even people freed from prison after so many years experience anxiety. Freedom is new to them. It scares them. People being released from the hospital after a long stay experience anxiety. They have become used to the hospital. The outside world is a change, is scary.

There is even the story about the man who won the lottery. He had serious heart problems. He didn't know when he won because he was in the hospital. The family had the ticket and they went to his cardiologist and said, "Hey, we have a problem. We're afraid that when he finds out he won, the shock could kill him, his heart's so weak." The cardiologist said, "Yes, you're right. The shock might have killed him. Let me handle this. I'll break it to him gradually." So the cardiologist, in making his normal rounds, just struck up a conversation with the man and injected, "What would you do if you ever hit the big one?" The man laughed. "Doc, I never win anything. I've been playing the lottery for years and never even got a sniff. I'll never hit a big one." But the cardiologist kept pressing him, asking what he would do if he did hit the lottery. The man thought for a moment, then said, "Well, Doc, one thing I would definitely do. You've taken such good care of me, I think I owe you my life. If I did hit, I'd give you half." And the cardiologist keeled over with a heart attack.

Change is hard. None of us codependents just become open to change. And none of us just decide that we're going to grow. Most of us kick, scream, battle, drive ourselves totally crazy, beat ourselves into the ground until we finally agree to try change.

I worked with a lot of addicts, and not just alcohol and other substance addicts. I mean overeaters, credit card junkies, gamblers...You name it. They see what they need to do, where they have to go. It's a pretty short, straight line. But—like all of us— they go around the block, into the next county, the next state, the next street, and when they finally can't go any more, they're so sick and tired, they finally walk that straight line. Why? Because it isn't easy. It requires change, giving up the familiar. But in the familiar, no matter how unhealthy it is, we have the illusion that we can control things. We convince ourselves that things aren't as bad as they feel, that all we need is time, a few minor adjustments, and then we'll be OK. When we're finally sick and tired of being sick and tired, we get in touch with just how insane things have become. We call that our dysfunctionality; we get in touch with that. We realize that we are dysfunctional, our families are dysfunctional, the whole world is dysfunctional. We mourn that. And then we become ready to try change and growth.

I'll share a last example of this: a person in a rotten relationship. We're not stupid. Usually we know when a relationship is dead, is unhealthy for us, causing us all kinds of pain. Yet we say things like, "I'll go when the kids are eighteen. I don't want to upset them." We're suffering, but we're afraid of upsetting the kids, upsetting our families, upsetting the way we were brought up, our family systems. And we beat ourselves to death. We martyr ourselves. We make ourselves into victims. And we shame ourselves because we don't want to upset anyone else. So who do you hurt the most? You. Zip. Period. You.

Continuing with the example, change *is* hard. It's not easy to walk away from a relationship that you've invested in and that reflects everything you've ever been taught by your Family of Origin, your culture, your religion, your peer groups, and the media. Which is why we said that, before you begin to try to change, build your base. Don't go on your journey alone. Develop a recovery family. Use your recovery tools. Connect with other people making the same journey. In recovery circles, we use a little symbol, an illustration, to guide us into change and growth.

THE RECOVERY TRIANGLE

We call the symbol the Recovery Triangle. Each side of the figure represents a core factor in recovery: your Higher Power; your Recovery Family; and relationship. Or, to put it succinctly: faith, family, relationship. Now, by relationship, we mean your relationship with life, with the fundamental concepts of life. We need to keep that in mind. We do not define relationship by the old tunnel vision definition; relationship means more than having interaction with just a person or persons. Relationship means how you interact with life itself.

These three components of the triangle make up a total person. If you eliminate any one of the three, you experience codependency. For example, if you eliminate faith, you may be in a recovery family, but recovery will be difficult, if not impossible, because you do not have faith that any process will work for you. On the other hand, if you have the element of faith in a Higher Power, no matter how you define that power, your recovery family gives you support and you relate to life, drawing lessons from all the relationships you experience, whether with people or events. In short, you learn from all areas of life, and you have faith that it will work.

For some, as we already noted, the concepts of Higher Power and faith might be tough to swallow. I suggest reading an explanation of the Twelve Steps. There are all sorts of versions in book stores, especially stores that specialize in recovery literature. But all versions are essentially the same. They all explain that many of us struggle with these concepts because our experiences were so bad—maybe are still so bad—that we just cannot accept the idea of a Higher Power or faith. But, further, the beauty of the Twelve Steps is that you really do not have to accept anything. All you need do is try. Start the work. Then, if you benefit, take the next step. In other words, you get paid as you go, so to speak. Don't try to analyze what you're doing, what the Steps prescribe, how they work. Just try them. See what happens. The concepts of Higher Power and faith become clearer from there.

But we make can your approach even simpler. There is what is called the HOW of the program, which we touched on before.

HONESTY, OPENNESS, WILLINGNESS—HOW

Now, please, note the order of the words and initials. It's not WOH. It's HOW. The first step in all growth is shame reduction work. That comes from honesty. And a lot of what we know about honesty in regard to this program comes from the Big Book of AA. By the way, if you're still hung up about that, still saying

"Hey, I'm not an alcoholic, what does that book have to do with me?", let me remind you again that the Big Book lays out the precepts, the model, that *has been adapted* to treating all sorts of psychological and emotional problems. And let me say again that if you have a problem thinking of yourself as an addict, think of an addict as someone who lives in fear, as opposed to love—someone who is not happy with life. That is what codependency is all about. That is why I like the Big Book and refer to it and quote from it so often.

The Big Book was basically put together by a bunch of drunks. They were desperate. Traditional medicine couldn't help them. So Dr. Bob and Bill W. and the others in the earliest groups got together and hung on to each other, and out of their struggles and pain came some concepts. They all put those concepts down in the Big Book, which is why there is no author listed. From the pain of a group came the book. To me, it's a sacred book; it saved my own life. It offers the gift of life in its principles. Its first principle is shame reduction, which is accomplished by honesty. As AA still emphasizes today—as all Twelve Step programs define themselves: "It's an honest program." And also remember the other saying: You are only as sick as your secrets.

So, to start your recovery, you strive for honesty. The more honest you become, the clearer you become, the cleaner you become, the more peaceful you become. Oh—and don't get hung up on "total" honesty. It's a rare person who achieves that—if anyone ever does. The program asks for Progress, Not Perfection. And, again, you start by trying.

If you follow a Twelve Step method, you will attempt to start with an honest inventory of yourself. It's called Step Four. You basically write out a personal history. We already covered some of this in journaling. There are no hard and fast rules to it. Basically, you just try to get things out on paper. This is another area where a Twelve Step book can give excellent guidance. The purpose of the exercise is to learn about yourself: your history, patterns, emotions, traumas, secrets, guilts…You are striving for self-knowledge.

There are many ways in which this process works. For example, a person I know never identified himself as a controlling person. He thought of "controlling" people as those who demanded things. In doing his inventory, he finally saw that he tried so much to please other people. Often he said yes to things, swallowed feelings, did what other people wanted, just so he could please them. And he realized: he did this in order to *control* them, to get them to like him. So he identified control as an issue to work on.

Another thing, you might do a personal inventory more than once. Most people do. In my own case, I did my first one, as a Fourth Step, in 1978. I was as honest as I could be. I did another inventory in 1982—and noticed that I was a hell of a lot more honest. Why? Because of the second part of the HOW: Openness.

Gaining knowledge about ourselves is one thing. But it is only one level. Openness is like the second level. We become open to learn from all areas of our lives. Some say that when that happens, when we add openness to a searching honesty, the process begins to take on a life of its own. And don't forget: it is a *healing* process. It will not hurt you. It evolves. As you become more open, you will learn more about yourself. And you will not see anything about yourself until you are ready to handle it. Take, for example, people who have serious abuse issues, maybe sexual abuse, even incest. They have buried the experiences, forgotten them, at least consciously. As they begin this process, become more open, the experiences come back to them—so they can finally face them and learn from them. Please note, though, that you are not working this process in a vacuum. Do not just sit down and take this little part of this book and say, "Hey, I'll start here and see what happens." You might not be able to handle what you bring up, which is why you develop your recovery family and arrest your addictions and have professional help available at arm's length in case you need it.

The Honesty and Openness, when coupled with a *Willingness* to learn and grow, complete the HOW of the program. You are honest—you learn. You open up more—your knowledge expands from other sources. Then you become willing to grow—you make the effort consciously to accept GOD—Good, Orderly, Direction. And please do not confuse *willingness* with *will power*. From my own experience with my food addiction, I can tell you that will power is kill power. You decide that you're just going to put your foot down, stop your codependent behaviors by sheer force of will alone. It doesn't work that way. You build your recovery system, including connecting to other people in recovery, and then you do the HOW and let things happen at their own pace. This same principle is reflected in many philosophies: When you are ready, a teacher will appear. HOW makes you ready.

And, please, don't complicate this process. Dr. Bob of AA probably said this best. It was way back around the 1940's when AA was having one of its first conventions. Dr. Bob was actually very sick, near death, yet he asked to address the convention. He came from his death bed and took the podium. His entire address was: "For God's sake, keep it simple."

If you have a mind to try this program, just do it. Don't analyze it. Don't try to figure out where it will lead you. Don't compare yourself with other people doing it. Don't put a time limit on it. Don't try to fit it into a pre-set format. Be honest. Be open. Be willing. Let go.

OWNERSHIP

The man I mentioned above who discovered control as one of his issues also discovered something else as he worked his program. He learned something about the concept of ownership. In this case, it didn't come from a written inventory, but from attending a Codependents Anonymous meeting. It happened while one of the group was sharing one of her experiences. She had just moved to the area from a different part of the country. She told of how she at first saw things in her new environment as depressing and strange. Then she opened up one day and saw things differently. For example, where she had come from, cities and developments were fairly new, there were virtually no old buildings. Her new location had many old structures, which she saw as depressing. However, when she opened up, became willing to look at things differently, she appreciated the history of the old structures, part of the culture of her new environment.

Just hearing that triggered something in the man. He realized that when he looked back in his life, he mostly focused on the negative. For example, in high school, he had bad experiences with a couple of teachers. When he thought of high school, he thought of them. Automatically. Like an addiction. In fact, he learned later that he was caught in this negative-view addiction; negativity is a sign of codependency. But in the meeting, hearing the woman, he suddenly realized that he could focus on the good things in his past, the positive. He could *choose* to do that. Or, to put it in different terms, he could finally take "ownership" for his own actions and feelings.

Now, he didn't get to that point, to that realization, automatically. It took work, working his personal program. The program helped him process the negative feelings in his past, "defuse" them, in a sense, and permit him to see the good in his past. Listening to the woman in the meeting triggered the realization that he could now choose, now take ownership for the present.

Ownership comes from openness, because openness simply means that everything in life is your teacher. If you do not take ownership for your present circumstances, all you are doing is renting space in your head to someone or some thing or some institution that hurt you ten, twenty, thirty years ago, or more. You are a prisoner of your past, instead of learning from it and moving on. If you do not take ownership, you get stuck in the Blame Game. You walk around with all kind of resentment and anger inside of you. You become your issues. And that is the essence of codependency, with its depression, anxiety, and addictions.

I am not saying that it is easy to let go of the past. It is not easy to let an ex-wife, ex-husband, the child who was driving you insane, or someone who perpetrated abuse on you to become your teacher. It is not easy to let someone you don't like become your teacher. It is not easy to let death or trauma or serious abuse or something else horrible become your teacher. But you do not have to like your teachers in life. We said before, some of them might drive you crazy. But, from the point of view of ownership, you have a choice. You can choose to continue playing victim, playing the Blame Game, and being miserable—which is ironic, since it doesn't make any difference whatsoever to those who hurt you in the past. Or you can say, "OK, I couldn't do anything about what was happening then and how I felt about it, but I can take responsibility for what I do with it now." That's called ownership. And, if you want to change, you get HOW: Honest, Open, Willing.

Many of us in recovery discover something about this process. It seems to take on a life of its own. Where change was so scary for us before, it actually becomes fun—and rewarding. My wife was a nurse. She had never considered any other career, even though she was losing her enthusiasm for it. She considered a change. It was scary. But she went through with it. She became a travel agent. And she loved it, traveling to all sorts of places to check them out, enjoying things she never considered before. In my own case, I remember once driving to church in a storm. I was brought up Catholic, and, at that time, there wasn't much of a spirit of ecumenism. They basically told you that other Churches were strange, negative places. But there I was, driving in a storm, trying to make it to my Catholic parish, and I realized just how hazardous my trip was going to be. Just about then, I passed another church, of Protestant denomination, and I decided to attend services there. As I suspected, I found out that the old tapes playing in my head were wrong. Worshiping in that church was a pleasant experience. After all, we were all praying to the same God, and I got a sense of fellowship with a whole new congregation of worshippers.

THE GREATEST BOOK YOU'LL EVER READ

In my lecture series, I close by telling my audience about the greatest book they can ever possibly read. And I say it this way: "The greatest book you'll ever read is YOU." YOU. Each and every one of us is like a book in the making, in process. Or, if you prefer, use another analogy: We are like flowers, constantly growing, constantly opening and blooming. Be open to your growth, to your story as it unfolds. People come into your life. Some stay. Some leave. Things happen. Things change. It is all there for one purpose: so you can learn. Learn and move on.

Learn from your personal story as it has been written so far. Embrace every aspect of your history, no matter how painful that is for you at first. Don't try to do it alone. In my own case, now that I finally understand that recovery is a process, an ongoing process, I really see the value of my recovery system. I still attend a codependency group and an Overeaters Anonymous group. Even when I'm traveling, in whatever city, I can look up the local groups and attend the meetings. So I'm never alone in "writing" and embracing my personal story. And once you start learning from the part of your story that is already written, the past, you also start learning from the present. In the Twelve Step program, you help this along by taking a daily inventory, by reflecting on each day. As I said very early in this book, what I like about the Twelve Step method is that it gives you something *to do*. It is not just an intellectual exercise. It changes you at the gut level.

I also tell my lecture groups not to force their story. I remind them of that gem of wisdom from ALANON, the slogan, INCH BY INCH. I tell them about a guy I knew way back when I worked in a rehab center. His name was Frank. He was very old. He had been an active alcoholic for most of his life. He finally got sober and into recovery, and some of the other people in the center would try to push him along. But Frank would tell them, "Hey, it took me 72 years to work Step One and that's enough. I'm not drinking. My life's a little saner. That's enough. Let me die in peace." We would laugh at that. He was reminding us to accept being where we were at, not to force things. After he died, we'd be at meetings at the center and occasionally the door would blow open and we'd joke and say, "There's Frank. He's back to remind us to keep it simple, don't force it." As codependents, we need that reminder. We are addicted to forcing things. We try to organize everything—including confusion.

I say to my groups that when I was in my 20's I was a sick dude. I had all the answers. That's an amazing place to be.

Nobody could tell me anything. Then I got to my 30's and found all the questions. I'd drive myself nuts trying to find the answers. In my 40's I realized that some of the questions had answers and some didn't. Now, in my 50's, I finally learned, "So what? Don't force things. Don't try to figure it all out and organize it." I hear that in your 60's it really gets exciting because then you don't give a damn one way or another. You just work on you and trust that everything else will fall into place.

In closing, I just want to share one last story, about the ninety-year-old priest I told you about before, one of my teachers when I was a seminarian. He was ninety-nine when he died, and two hours before he died, on his death bed, he asked one of the seminarians who was with him to run to the library and pick up some books for him. The seminarian gave a stunned response: "Why?" The old priest said, "Because there are a couple of things I still want to learn about myself yet. I just want to discover those things about myself before I die this afternoon."

You see, that's the thing about your personal story, about the book that is unfolding in you: It doesn't end. If you are Honest, Open, and Willing, you will learn till the day, till the very second, you die. Along the way, if you put together your personal recovery program, you will grow past codependency. You will experience serenity and the joy of living. That is the Promise of recovery.

Trust the process. The process works.